Anonymous

Where the old and the new Versions differ

The actual Changes in the Authorized and Revised New Testament

Anonymous

Where the old and the new Versions differ
The actual Changes in the Authorized and Revised New Testament

ISBN/EAN: 9783337117764

Printed in Europe, USA, Canada, Australia, Japan

Cover: Foto ©ninafisch / pixelio.de

More available books at **www.hansebooks.com**

WHERE THE OLD

AND THE

NEW VERSIONS DIFFER.

THE ACTUAL CHANGES

IN THE

AUTHORIZED AND REVISED NEW TESTAMENT.

PRINTED IN PARALLEL COLUMNS.

NEW YORK:
ANSON D. F. RANDOLPH & COMPANY,
900 Broadway, cor. 20th Street.

COPYRIGHT, 1881, BY
ANSON D. F. RANDOLPH & COMPANY.

Edward O. Jenkins, Printer and Stereotyper,
20 North William St., N. Y.

The object of the present publication is to show at once the actual differences between the Authorized and the Revised Versions of the New Testament. It is issued without note or comment, that it may be a ready help, not only to the general reader, but to the devout student of the Scriptures.

WHERE THE OLD

AND THE

NEW VERSIONS DIFFER.

S. MATTHEW.

1. 25   ST. MATTHEW.   S. MATTHEW.   1

Chap.	Authorized Version.	Revised Version.
1 11	—about the time they were carried away to Babylon :	—at the time of the carrying away to Babylon.
12	And after they were brought to Babylon,	And after the carrying away to Babylon,
17	Christ	—the Christ.
18	When as his mother Mary was espoused to Joseph,	When his mother Mary had been betrothed to Joseph,
19	a just man	a righteous man
20	—while he thought	—when he thought
21	—for he shall save	—for it is he that shall save
22	—all this was done	—all this is come to pass
	—spoken of the Lord by the prophet,	—spoken by the Lord through the prophet,
24	Then Joseph being raised from sleep	And Joseph arose from his sleep
25	—brought forth her first-born son ;	—brought forth a son :

Chap.		Authorized Version.	Revised Version.
2	2	—for we have seen	—for we saw his star
	3	—had heard these things,	—heard it,
	4	—demanded of them	—inquried of them
	6	And thou Bethlehem, *in* the land of Juda, art not the least among the princes of Juda: for out of thee shall come a Governor, that shall rule my people Israel.	And thou Bethlehem, land of Judah, art in no wise least among the princes of Judah: For out of thee shall come forth a governor, which shall be shepherd of my people Israel.
	7	—enquired of them diligently	—learned of them carefully
	8	—search diligently for the young child;	—search out carefully concerning the young child;
	13	—be thou there until I bring thee word:	—be thou there until I tell thee:
	15	—of the Lord by the prophet,	—by the Lord through the prophet,
	16	—slew all the children	—slew all the male children
	22	—notwithstanding being warned of God	—and being warned of God
	23	He shall be called a Nazarene.	—that he should be called a Nazarene
3	7	O generation of vipers,	Ye offspring of vipers,
	10	And now also	And even now
	12	—throughly purge his floor,	throughly cleanse his threshing-floor;
	14	But John forbad him,	But John would have hindered him,
	16	—out of the water:	—from the water;

Chap.	Authorized Version.	Revised Version.
16	—like a dove and lighting upon him:	—as a dove, and coming upon him;
17	—voice from heaven,	—voice out of the heavens,
4 12	—when Jesus had heard that John was cast into prison, he departed into Galilee;	—when he heard that John was delivered up, he withdrew into Galilee
15	—by the way of the sea,	Toward the sea,
16	—saw great light;	Saw a great light,
24	—they brought unto him all sick people that were taken with divers diseases and torments, and those which were possessed with devils, and those which were lunatick, and those that had the palsy;	—they brought unto him all that were sick, holden with divers diseases and torments, possessed with devils, and epileptic, and palsied;
5 1	—when he was set,	—when he had sat down,
9	—children of God.	—sons of God.
11	—men shall revile you,	—men shall reproach you,
15	—light a candle	—light a lamp,
	—on a candlestick	—on the stand;
18	—till all be fulfilled.	—till all things be accomplished.
22	—without a cause	*omitted.*
23	—if thou bring thy gift to the altar,	If therefore thou art offering thy gift at the altar,
25	—lest at any time	—lest haply
27	—by them of old time,	*omitted.*

Chap.	Authorized Version.	Revised Version.
29	—if thy right eye offend thee,	—if thy right eye causeth thee to stumble,
30	—if thy right hand offend thee,	—if thy right hand causeth thee to stumble,
	—should be cast into hell.	—go into hell.
31	It hath been said,	It was said also,
32	—causeth her to commit adultery:	—maketh her an adulteress:
33	—it hath been said by them of old time,	—it was said to them of old time,
37	—let your communication	—let your speech
	—cometh of evil.	—is of the evil one.
39	—resist not evil:	—Resist not him that is evil:
44	—bless them that curse you, do good to them that hate you,	} *omitted.*
	—despitefully use you	*omitted.*
45	—children of your Father	—sons of your Father
47	—do not even the publicans so!	—do not even the Gentiles the same?
48	Be ye therefore perfect,	Ye therefore shall be perfect,
6 1	—do not your alms before men,	—do not your righteousness before men,
2	They have their reward.	They have received their reward.
4	—shall reward thee openly.	—shall recompense thee.
5	—love to pray standing	—love to stand and pray
6	—reward thee openly.	—recompense thee.

Chap.	Authorized Version.	Revised Version.
7	But when ye pray, —as the heathen do:	And in praying —as the Gentiles do
10	—in earth, as it is in heaven.	—as in heaven, so on earth.
12	—as we forgive	—as we also have forgiven
13	—lead us not —deliver us from evil For thine is the kingdom, and the power, and the glory, for ever. Amen.	—bring us not —deliver us from the evil one. } *omitted.*
16	—that they may appear unto men —they have their reward	—that they may be seen of men —they have received their reward.
18	—that thou appear not unto men —reward thee openly.	—that thou be not seen of men —recompense thee.
22	—light of the body	—lamp of the body
25	—Take no thought	—Be not anxious
26	—yet your heavenly Father —much better	—and your heavenly Father —of much more value
27	—by taking thought	—by being anxious
28	—why take ye thought for raiment?	—why are ye anxious concerning raiment?
31	Therefore take no thought,	Be not therefore anxious,
34	Take therefore no thought for the morrow: for the morrow shall take	Be not therefore anxious for the morrow: for the morrow will be anxious for itself.

Chap.		Authorized Version.	Revised Version.
		thought for the things of itself.	
7	2	—measured to you again.	—measured unto you.
	6	—lest they trample	—lest haply they trample
	13	—the strait gate:	—the narrow gate:
	14	Because strait is the gate, and narrow is the way,	For narrow is the gate, and straitened the way,
	28	—the people	—the multitudes
8	9	For I am a man under authority,	For I also am a man under authority,
	12	—children of the kingdom	—sons of the kingdom
	25	—his disciples came to him, and awoke him,	—they came to him, and awoke him,
	31	—suffer us to go away	—send us away
	33	—they that kept them	—they that fed them
9	8	—they marvelled,	—they were afraid,
	9	—passed forth	—passed by
		—the receipt of custom:	—the place of toll:
	13	—I will have mercy,	—I desire mercy,
		—to repentance	*omitted*.
	16	No man putteth a piece of new cloth unto an old garment, for that which is put in to fill it up taketh from the garment, and the rent is made worse.	And no man putteth a piece of undressed cloth upon an old garment; for that which should fill it up taketh from the garment, and a worse rent is made.
	17	—old bottles:	—old wine-skins:
		—the bottles break, and	—the skins burst, and

Chap.		Authorized Version.	Revised Version.
		the wine runneth out, and the bottles perish :	the wine is spilled, and the skins perish
		—new bottles,	—fresh wine-skins,
	21	If I may	If I do
	22	—good comfort ;	—good cheer ;
	23	—the minstrels and the people making a noise,	—the flute-players, and the crowd making a tumult,
	25	—the people	—the crowd
	30	—straightly charged	—strictly charged
	31	But they, when they were departed,	But they went forth,
	36	—because they fainted	—because they were distressed
10	3	—and Lebbæus, whose surname was Thaddæus ;	—and Thaddæus ;
	4	Simon the Canaanite	Simon the Cananæan,
	5	Go not into the way	Go not into any way
	9	Provide neither gold nor silver	Get you no gold nor silver
	10	Nor scrip for your journey,	No wallet for your journey,
		—nor yet staves :	nor staff :
	11	—enquire who in it is worthy ;	—search out who in it is worthy ;
	18	—for a testimony against them	—for a testimony to them
	19	—take no thought	—be not anxious
	23	—flee ye into another :	—flee into the next :
11	3	Art thou he that should come,	Art thou he that cometh,

Chap.	Authorized Version.	Revised Version.
4	Go and shew John again those things	Go your way and tell John the things
5	—the gospel	—good tidings
6	—shall not be offended in me.	—shall find none occasion of stumbling in me.
7	—as they departed,	—as these went their way,
11	—notwithstanding he that is least	—yet he that is but little
12	—and the violent	—and men of violence
17	—we have mourned unto you, and ye have not lamented.	—we wailed, and ye did not mourn.
19	But wisdom is justified of her children.	And wisdom is justified by her works.
23	And thou, Capernaum, which art exalted unto heaven, shalt be brought down to hell:	And thou, Capernaum, shalt thou be exalted unto heaven? thou shalt go down into Hades:
25	—wise and prudent,	—wise and understanding,
26	Even so, Father: for so it seemed good in thy sight.	—yea, Father, for so it was well-pleasing in thy sight.
27	—are delivered	—have been delivered
	—will reveal him.	—willeth to reveal him.
12 1	—through the corn;	—through the cornfields;
6	—in this place is one greater than the temple.	—one greater than the temple is here.
7	—I will have mercy,	—I desire mercy

Chap.	Authorized Version.	Revised Version.
8	—Lord even of the Sabbath day	—lord of the Sabbath.
12	—better than a sheep?	—of more value than a sheep!
	—to do well	—to do good
14	—held a council	—took counsel
15	But when Jesus knew it,	And Jesus perceiving it
	—great multitudes	—many
21	—shall the Gentiles trust.	—shall the Gentiles hope.
23	—all the people	—all the multitudes
24	—this fellow	—this man
27	—your children	—your sons
29	Or else how can one enter	Or how can one enter
31	—All manner of sin	Every sin
	—Holy Ghost	Spirit
34	O generation of vipers,	Ye offspring of vipers,
35	—the good treasure of the heart	—his good treasure
43	—dry places	—waterless places
45	—is worse	—becometh worse
46	—desiring to speak	—seeking to speak
13 7	—sprung up	—grew up
12	—more abundance	—abundance
15	—lest at any time	—lest haply
	—should be converted,	—should turn again,
19	—then cometh the wicked one, and catcheth away	—then cometh the evil one, and snatcheth away
	—which received seed	—that was sown
20	—he that received the	—he that was sown

Chap.	Authorized Version.	Revised Version.
	seed into stony places,	upon the rocky places,
21	—by and by he is offended.	—straightway he stumbleth.
22	—he also that received seed among the thorns	—And he that was sown among the thorns,
23	But he that received seed into the good ground	And he that was sown upon the good ground,
29	—lest while ye gather	—lest haply while ye gather
32	—it is the greatest among herbs,	—it is greater than the herbs,
35	—which have been kept secret	—hidden
36	Then Jesus sent the multitude away,	Then he left the multitudes,
	—Declare unto us	—Explain unto us
41	—things that offend,	—things that cause stumbling,
43	—Who hath ears to hear,	—He that hath ears,
48	—drew to shore	—drew up on the beach;
49	—the just,	—the righteous
51	Jesus saith unto them, Yea, Lord.	*omitted.* Yea.
52	—which is instructed unto	—who hath been made a disciple to
54	And when he was come	And coming
14 1	—the fame of Jesus,	—the report concerning Jesus,
2	—and therefore mighty works do shew	—and therefore do these powers work in him.

Chap.	Authorized Version.	Revised Version.
	forth themselves in him.	
6	—birthday was kept	—birthday came
	—before them	—in the midst
8	—being before instructed of her mother,	—being put forward by her mother,
13	—people	—multitudes
14	—was moved with compassion toward them,	—he had compassion on them
20	—of the fragments that remained	—that which remained over of the broken pieces,
24	—tossed with waves :	—distressed by the waves ;
26	—It is a spirit	—It is an apparition ;
35	—had knowledge of him,	—knew him,
36	—were made perfectly whole	—were made whole.
15 1	—which were of Jerusalem,	—from Jerusalem
3	—by your tradition ?	—because of your tradition ?
4	For God commanded, saying,	For God said,
	—He that curseth father or mother,	—He that speaketh evil of father or mother
5	But ye say, Whosoever shall say to his father or his mother, It is a gift, by whatsoever thou mightest be profited by me ;	But ye say, Whosoever shall say to his father or his mother, That wherewith thou mightest have been profited by me is given to God ; he
6	And honour not his	

Chap.	Authorized Version.	Revised Version.
	father or his mother, he shall be free. Thus have ye made the commandment of God of none effect by your tradition.	shall not honour his father. And ye have made void the word of God because of your tradition.
8	—draweth nigh unto me with their mouth, and	} *omitted*.
9	—teaching for doctrines	—Teaching as their doctrines
12	—after they heard	—when they heard
14	—they be blind leaders of the blind.	—they are blind guides.
	—into the ditch.	—into a pit.
17	Do not ye yet understand,	Perceive ye not,
19	—blasphemies	—railings
27	Truth, Lord	Yea, Lord
32	—lest they faint	—lest haply they faint
33	—the wilderness,	—a desert place,
37	—and they took up of the broken meat that was left	—and they took up that which remained over of the broken pieces,
39	—Magdala	—Magadan
16 2	—the sky	—the heaven
3	O ye hypocrites,	*omitted*.
4	—the sign of the prophet Jonas.	—the sign of Jonah.
7	It is because we have taken no bread.	We took no bread.
9	—understand	—perceive
12	—doctrine	—teaching

Chap.	Authorized Version.	Revised Version.
13	—Whom do men say that I the Son of man am?	Who do men say that the Son of man is?
14	—Some say thou art John the Baptist:	Some say John the Baptist;
18	—the gates of hell	—the gates of Hades
20	—Jesus the Christ.	—the Christ.
22	—this shall not be	—this shall never be
23	—an offence	—a stumblingblock
	—thou savourest not	—thou mindest not
26	—and lose his own soul?	—and forfeit his life?
	—in exchange for his soul?	—in exchange for his life?
27	—reward every man	—render unto every man
28	—There be some standing here,	—There be some of them that stand here,
	—shall not taste of death,	—shall in no wise taste of death,
17 4	—let us make here three tabernacles;	—I will make here three tabernacles;
11	Elias truly shall first come,	Elijah indeed cometh,
15	—lunatick	—epileptic
	—and sore vexed:	—and suffereth grievously:
17	—how long shall I suffer you?	—how long shall I bear with you?
18	And Jesus rebuked the devil;	And Jesus rebuked him;
	—the child was cured	—the boy was cured
20	—your unbelief:	—your little faith:

Chap.	Authorized Version.	Revised Version.
21	Howbeit this kind goeth not out but by prayer and fasting	} omitted.
22	—betrayed	—delivered up
24	—tribute money	—the half-shekel
25	—Jesus prevented him,	—Jesus spake first to him,
	—custom	—toll
	—their own children	—their sons
27	—lest we should offend them,	—lest we cause them to stumble,
	—a piece of money:	—a shekel:
18 1	At the same time	In that hour
3	—Except ye be converted,	Except ye turn
6	. But whoso shall offend one of these little ones which believe in me, it were better for him that a millstone were hanged about his neck, and that he were drowned in the depth of the sea.	—but whoso shall cause one of these little ones which believe on me to stumble, it is profitable for him that a great millstone should be hanged about his neck, and that he should be sunk in the depth of the sea.
7	—because of offences!	—because of occasions of stumbling!
	—that offences come;	—that the occasions come;
	—the offence cometh!	—the occasion cometh!
8	—offend thee,	—causeth thee to stumble,

Chap.	Authorized Version.	Revised Version.
8	—everlasting fire.	—the eternal fire.
9	—offend thee,	—causeth thee to stumble,
	—into hell fire	—into hell of fire.
10	Take heed	See
11	For the Son of man is come to save that which was lost.	omitted.
15	—trespass against thee,	—sin against thee,
17	—neglect	—refuse
	—an heathen man	—the Gentile
23	—take account of his servants.	—make a reckoning with his servants.
27	—loosed him,	—released him,
29	—fell down at his feet	—fell down
	—I will pay thee all.	—I will pay thee.
30	—the debt	—that which was due.
32	—thou desiredst me:	—thou besoughtest me:
33	—compassion	—mercy
	—pity	—mercy
35	—If ye from your hearts forgive not every one his brother their trespasses.	—if ye forgive not every one his brother from your hearts.
19 10	—good	—expedient
16	—Good Master,	—Master,
17	—Why callest thou me good? there is none good but one, that is, God:	—Why askest thou me concerning that which is good? One there is who is good:
18	—Thou shalt do no murder,	—Thou shalt not kill,

Chap.	Authorized Version.	Revised Version.
20	—All these things have I kept from my youth up:	—All these things have I observed:
23	—a rich man shall hardly enter	It is hard for a rich man to enter
29	—or wife	*omitted.*
20 6	—standing idle,	—standing;
7	—and whatsoever is right, that shall ye receive.	*omitted.*
10	—should have received	—would receive
11	—goodman of the house,	—householder
12	—wrought	—spent
	—burden and heat of the day.	—burden of the day and the scorching heat.
14	—I will give unto this last, even as unto thee.	—it is my will to give unto this last, even as unto thee.
16	—for many be called, but few chosen.	*omitted.*
18	—betrayed	—delivered
19	—he shall rise again.	—he shall be raised up.
22	—the cup that I shall drink of,	—the cup that I am about to drink?
	—and to be baptized with the baptism that I am baptized with?	*omitted.*
23	—and be baptized with the baptism that I am baptized with:	*omitted.*
	—but it shall be given to them	—but it is for them

Chap.	Authorized Version.	Revised Version.
24	—against	—concerning
25	—the princes of the Gentiles exercise dominion over them, and they that are great exercise authority upon them.	—the rulers of the Gentiles lord it over them, and their great ones exercise authority over them
26	—will be great	—would become great
27	And whosoever will be chief among you, let him be your servant:	—and whosoever would be first among you shall be your servant:
34	—had compassion on them,	—being moved with compassion,
21 4	All this was done,	Now this is come to pass,
6	—commanded	—appointed
7	—and they set him thereon.	—and he sat thereon.
8	—a very great multitude	—the most part of the multitude
10	—moved,	—stirred,
15	—they were sore displeased,	—they were moved with indignation,
19	—in the way,	—by the way side,
	—presently	—immediately
20	—How soon is the fig tree withered away!	—How did the fig tree immediately wither away?
21	—removed	—taken up
26	—we fear the people;	—we fear the multitude;
27	—We cannot tell.	—We know not.
29	—repented,	—repented himself,

2

Chap.	Authorized Version.	Revised Version.
32	—repented not afterward,	—did not even repent yourselves afterward,
33	—a far country.	—another country.
34	—time of the fruit	—season of the fruits
	—that they might receive the fruits of it.	—to receive his fruits.
38	—let us seize on	—take
39	—they caught him,	—they took him,
40	—cometh,	—shall come,
41	—wicked men,	—miserable men,
42	—is become	—was made
	—this is the Lord's doing,	This was from the Lord.
44	—broken :	—broken to pieces :
	—it will grind him to powder.	—it will scatter him as dust.
22 2	—marriage	—marriage feast
3	—wedding :	—marriage feast :
4	—prepared	—made ready
	—marriage.	—marriage feast.
6	—the remnant took his servants,	—the rest laid hold on his servants,
	—spitefully,	—shamefully,
7	But when the king heard thereof he was wroth :	But the king was wroth ;
9	—the highways,	—the partings of the highways,
	—marriage.	—marriage feast.
10	—furnished	—filled
15	—entangle	—ensnare

Chap.		Authorized Version.	Revised Version.
	16	—any man:	—any one:
	22	When they had heard these words,	And when they heard it,
	25	—having no issue,	—having no seed
	27	And last of all	And after them all
	30	—the angels of God in heaven.	—angels in heaven.
	33	—doctrine.	—teaching.
	35	—and saying,	*omitted.*
	39	And the second is like unto it,	And a second like unto it is this,
	44	—till I make thine enemies thy footstool?	Till I put thine enemies underneath thy feet?
23	4	For they bind	Yea, they bind
	6	—uppermost rooms	—chief place
	7	—greetings	—salutations
	8	—Master,	—teacher,
	12	—abased;	—humbled;
	14	Woe unto you scribes and Pharisees, hypocrites! for ye devour widows' houses, and for a pretence make long prayer: therefore ye shall receive the greater damnation.	*omitted.*
	18	—he is guilty.	—he is a debtor.
	19	Ye fools and blind:	Ye blind:
	23	—have omitted	—have left undone
	24	—which strain at a gnat, and swallow a camel.	—which strain out a gnat, and swallow the camel.

Chap.	Authorized Version.	Revised Version.
25	—full of	—full from
26	—cleanse first that which is within the cup	—cleanse first the inside of the cup
31	—ye be witnesses unto yourselves,	—ye witness to yourselves,
33	—generation of vipers, —damnation of hell?	—offspring of vipers, —judgment of hell?
35	—temple	—sanctuary
24 1	And Jesus went out, and departed from the temple:	And Jesus went out from the temple, and was going on his way;
4	—deceive you.	—lead you astray.
5	—deceive many.	—lead many astray.
7	—and pestilences,	*omitted.*
8	All these are the beginning of sorrows.	But all these things are the beginning of travail.
9	—deliver you up to be afflicted,	—deliver you up unto tribulation,
10	—be offended, —betray one another,	—stumble, —deliver up one another,
11	—shall deceive many.	—shall lead many astray.
12	—shall abound,	—shall be multiplied,
14	—witness	—testimony
15	—stand	—standing
17	—to take anything out of his house:	—to take out the things that are in his house:
18	—clothes.	—cloke.
21	—was not	—hath not been
24	—insomuch that, if it	—so as to lead astray, if

Chap.	Authorized Version.	Revised Version.
	were possible, they shall deceive the very elect.	possible, even the elect.
26	—desert;	—wilderness;
	—secret chambers;	—inner chambers;
27	—shineth	—is seen
32	Now learn a parable of the fig tree;	Now from the fig tree learn her parable:
	—is yet tender,	—is now become tender,
34	—fulfilled.	—accomplished.
36	—no, not the angels of heaven, but my Father only.	—not even the angels of heaven, neither the Son, but the Father only.
40	Then shall two be in the field;	Then shall two men be in the field;
42	—what hour	—on what day
43	—goodman	—master
	—broken up.	—broken through.
47	—he shall make him ruler over all his goods.	—he will set him over all that he hath.
48	—delayeth his coming;	—tarrieth;
50	—in a day when he looketh not for him, and in an hour that he is not aware of.	—in a day when he expecteth not, and in an hour when he knoweth not,
25 6	And at midnight there was a cry made, Behold, the bridegroom cometh: go ye out to meet him.	But at midnight there is a cry, Behold, the bridegroom! Come ye forth to meet him.
8	—for our lamps are gone out.	—for our lamps are going out.

Chap.	Authorized Version.	Revised Version.
9	But the wise answered, saying, Not so; lest there be not enough for us and you:	But the wise answered, saying, Peradventure there will not be enough for us and you:
10	—marriage:	—marriage feast:
13	—wherein the Son of man cometh.	} *omitted*.
14	For the kingdom of heaven is as a man travelling into a far country,	For it is as when a man going into another country,
15	—and straightway took his journey.	—and he went on his journey.
16	Then he that had received	Straightway he that received
21	—I will make thee ruler over (*Same in v.* 23)	I will set thee over
24	—strawed.	—scattered.
27	—exchangers,	—bankers,
	—usury.	—interest
40	—Inasmuch as ye have done it unto one of the least of these my brethren,	Inasmuch as ye did it unto one of these my brethren, even these least,
41	—everlasting fire,	—the eternal fire
46	—everlasting	—eternal
26 2	—is the feast of the passover,	—the passover cometh,
	—betrayed	—delivered up
3	—palace	—court
4	—consulted	—took counsel together

Chap.	Authorized Version.	Revised Version.
5	—Not on the feast day, lest there be an uproar among the people.	—Not during the feast, lest a tumult arise among the people.
7	—an alabaster box of very precious ointment,	—an alabaster cruse of exceeding precious ointment,
10	—understood it,	—perceiving it
12	—she did it for my burial.	—she did it to prepare me for burial.
15	—And they covenanted with him	—And they weighed unto him
16	—betray him.	—deliver him unto them.
17	—first day of the feast of unleavened bread	—first day of unleavened bread
20	—he sat down with the twelve.	—he was sitting at meat with the twelve disciples.
25	—Master, is it I ?	—Is it I, Rabbi ?
27	—the cup	—a cup,
28	—the new testament,	—the covenant,
31	—because of me	—in me
32	—after I am risen again,	—after I am raised up,
35	—Though I should die with thee,	—Even if I must die with thee,
37	—very heavy.	—sore troubled.
42	—if this cup may not pass away from me,	—if this cannot pass away,
48	—hold him fast.	—take him.
50	—wherefore art thou come ?	—do that for which thou art come.
53	—pray to my Father, —presently	—beseech my Father, —even now

Chap.		Authorized Version.	Revised Version.
	55	—a thief	—a robber
		—ye laid no hold on me.	—ye took me not.
	56	—was done,	—is come to pass,
	58	—high priest's palace	—court of the high priest,
		—the servants,	—the officers,
	60	But found none: yea, though many false witnesses came, yet found they none.	—and they found it not, though many false witnesses came.
		—At last came two false witnesses,	But afterward came two,
	61	—This fellow said,	This man said,
	66	—guilty	—worthy
	69	—the palace :	—the court :
		—of Galilee.	—the Galilæan.
	71	—fellow	—man
		—Jesus of Nazareth.	—Jesus the Nazarene.
27	5	—in the temple,	—into the sanctuary,
	9	—was valued,	—was priced,
		—they of the children of Israel did value	—certain of the children of Israel did price ;
	14	And he answered him to never a word ;	And he gave him no answer, not even to one word :
	15	—release unto the people a prisoner,	—release unto the multitude one prisoner,
	19	—when he was set down	—while he was sitting
		—just	—righteous
	23	—cried out the more,	—cried out exceedingly,
	24	—tumult was made,	—tumult was arising,
		—this just person :	—this righteous man :

Chap.	Authorized Version.	Revised Version.
27	—the common hall,	—the palace,
	—whole band of soldiers.	—whole band.
29	—bowed the knee before him,	—kneeled down before him,
32	—him they compelled to bear his cross.	—him they compelled to go with them, that he might bear his cross.
34	—vinegar	—wine
35	—that it might be fulfilled which was spoken by the prophet, They parted my garments among them, and upon my vesture did they cast lots.	omitted.
39	—reviled him,	—railed on him,
42	—If he be the King of Israel,	He is the King of Israel;
43	—if he will have him:	—if he desireth him:
44	—cast the same in his teeth.	—cast upon him the same reproach.
50	—the ghost.	—his spirit.
52	—many bodies of the saints which slept arose,	—many bodies of the saints that had fallen asleep were raised;
58	He went to Pilate, and begged the body of Jesus. Then Pilate commanded the body to be delivered.	—this man went to Pilate, and asked for the body of Jesus. Then Pilate commanded it to be given up.
62	—that followed the day of the preparation,	—which is the day after the Preparation,
64	—lest his disciples come by night,	—lest haply his disciples come

Chap.	Authorized Version.	Revised Version.
65	—a watch :	—a guard :
66	—and setting a watch.	—the guard being with them.
28 1	In the end of the sabbath,	Now late on the sabbath day,
2	—and came and rolled back the stone from the door,	—and came and rolled away the stone,
3	—countenance	—appearance
4	—the keepers did shake,	—the watchers did quake,
9	—as they went to tell his disciples,	} omitted.
	—held him by the feet,	—took hold of his feet,
11	—watch	—guard
	—done.	—come to pass.
14	—and secure you.	—and rid you of care.
15	—is commonly reported	—was spread abroad
	—until this day.	—and continueth until this day.
18	—all power is given	—All authority hath been given
19	—and teach all nations,	—and make disciples of all the nations,
20	—Amen.	*omitted.*

S. MARK.

Chap.		Authorized Version.	Revised Version.
1	2	As it is written in the prophets,	Even as it is written in Isaiah the prophet,
		—which shall prepare thy way before thee.	—Who shall prepare thy way;
	3	—Prepare ye the way of the Lord,	—Make ye ready the way of the Lord,
	4	John did baptize in the wilderness,	John came, who baptized in the wilderness
	6	—and with a girdle of skin	—and had a leathern girdle
	7	—one mightier than I	—he that is mightier than I,
	10	—opened,	—rent asunder,
		—like a dove	—as a dove
	11	—in whom	—in thee
	12	—immediately	—straightway
	14	—put in prison,	—delivered up,
		—the gospel of the kingdom of God,	—the gospel of God,
	16	Now as he walked by the sea of Galilee,	And passing along by the sea of Galilee,
	22	—doctrine:	—teaching:
	23	And there was	And straightway there was
	24	—Let us alone;	*omitted.*

Chap.	Authorized Version.	Revised Version.
27	—What thing is this? what new doctrine is this?	What is this? a new teaching!
28	And immediately his fame spread abroad	And the report of him went out straightway
30	—and anon	—and straightway
31	—and immediately the fever left her,	—and the fever left her,
35	—a solitary place,	—a desert place,
37	—All men seek for thee.	—All are seeking thee.
38	—Let us go	—Let us go elsewhere
42	—as soon as he had spoken,.	*omitted*.
43	And he straitly charged him, and forthwith sent him away;	And he strictly charged him, and straightway sent him out,
45	—to blaze abroad	—to spread abroad
2 2	—to receive them,	—for them,
	—preached	—spake
4	—the press,	—the crowd,
7	Why doth this man thus speak blasphemies? who can forgive sins but God only?	Why doth this man thus speak? he blasphemeth: who can forgive sins but one, even God?
14	—the receipt of custom,	—the place of toll,
16	—scribes and Pharisees	—scribes of the Pharisees,
	—How is it that he eateth and drinketh with publicans and sinners?	—He eateth and drinketh with publicans and sinners.

Chap.	Authorized Version.	Revised Version.
17	—to repentance.	*omitted.*
18	—used to fast :	—were fasting :
19	—children	—sons
20	—then shall they fast in those days.	—then will they fast in that day.
21	—new cloth	—undressed cloth
	—else the new piece that filleth it up taketh away from the old,	—else that which should fill it up taketh from it, the new from the old,
22	—old bottles :	—old wine-skins :
	—the wine is spilled, and the bottles will be marred :	—the wine perisheth, and the skins :
	—but new wine must be put into new bottles.	—but they put new wine into fresh wine-skins.
28	Therefore the Son of man	—so that the Son of man
3 4	—evil ?	—harm ?
5	—hardness	—hardening
	—whole as the other.	*omitted.*
9	—small ship	—little boat
	—multitude,	—crowd,
11	—when they saw him,	—whensoever they beheld him,
12	—he straitly charged them	—he charged them much
13	—whom he would :	—whom he himself would :
14	—ordained	—appointed
15	And to have power to	—and to have author-

Chap.	Authorized Version.	Revised Version.
	heal sicknesses, and to cast out devils:	ity to cast out devils:
18	—the Canaanite,	—the Canaæan,
19	—and they went into an house.	And he cometh into a house.
25	—cannot stand.	—will not be able to stand.
29	—but is in danger of eternal damnation:	—but is guilty of an eternal sin:
4 2	—doctrine,	—teaching,
4	—some fell by the way side, and the fowls of the air came and devoured it up.	—some seed fell by the way side, and the birds came and devoured it.
5	—stony	—rocky
	—depth	—deepness
8	—and did yield fruit that sprang up and increased;	and yielded fruit, growing up and increasing;
10	—the parable	—the parables.
11	—Unto you is given to know the mystery	—Unto you is given the mystery
12	—lest at any time they should be converted, and their sins should be forgiven them.	—lest haply they should turn again, and it should be forgiven them.
15	—that was sown in their hearts.	—which hath been sown in them.
	—stony ground;	—rocky place,
	—gladness;	—joy;
17	—and so endure but for a time:	—but endure for a while;
	—immediately they are offended.	—straightway they stumble.

Chap.	Authorized Version.	Revised Version.
18	—such as hear the word,	—these are they that have heard the word,
20	—and receive it,	—and accept it,
21	—candle	—lamp
	—candlestick?	—stand?
22	For there is nothing hid which shall not be manifested; neither was anything kept secret, but that it should come abroad.	For there is nothing hid, save that it should be manifested; neither was anything made secret, but that it should come to light.
24	—and unto you that hear shall more be given.	—and more shall be given unto you.
26	—into the ground;	—upon the earth;
29	—brought forth,	—ripe,
30	—or with what comparison shall we compare it?	—or in what parable shall we set it forth?
32	—fowls of the air	—birds of the heaven
34	—and when they were alone, he expounded all things to his disciples.	—but privately to his own disciples he expounded all things.
36	And when they had sent away the multitude,	And leaving the multitude,
37	—so that it was now full.	—insomuch that the boat was now filling.
38	And he was in the hinder part of the ship, asleep on a pillow:	And he himself was in the stern, asleep on the cushion:
39	—arose	—awoke

Chap.	Authorized Version.	Revised Version.
40	—how is it that ye have no faith?	—have ye not yet faith?
41	—What manner of man is this,	—who then is this,
5 3	—and no man could bind him, no, not with chains:	—and no man could any more bind him, no, not with a chain;
4	—plucked	—rent
	—neither could any man tame him.	—and no man had strength to tame him.
11	—nigh unto the mountains	—on the mountain side
12	And all the devils besought him,	And they besought him,
13	And forthwith Jesus gave them leave.	And he gave them leave.
	—ran violently down a steep place into the sea,	—rushed down the steep into the sea,
14	—And they went out to see what it was that was done.	And they came to see what it was that had come to pass.
17	And they began to pray him to depart out of their coasts.	And they began to beseech him to depart from their borders.
19	—Go home to thy friends,	—Go to thy house unto thy friends,
23	—that she may be healed, and she may live.	—that she may be made whole, and live.
30	—that virtue had gone out of him	—that the power proceeding from him had gone forth,
35	—there came from the	—they come from the

Chap.	Authorized Version.	Revised Version.
	ruler of the synagogue's house certain which said,	ruler of the synagogue's house, saying,
36	As soon as Jesus heard the word that was spoken,	But Jesus, not heeding the word spoken,
38	—and seeth the tumult, and them that wept and wailed greatly.	—and he beholdeth a tumult, and many weeping and wailing greatly.
39	—this ado,	—a tumult,
40	—father and mother of the damsel,	—father of the child and her mother
42	—And they were astonished with a great astonishment.	—And they were amazed straightway with a great amazement.
43	—straitly	—much
6 2	—that even such mighty works are wrought by his hands?	—and what mean such mighty works wrought by his hands?
9	But be shod with sandals; and not put on two coats.	—but to go shod with sandals: and, said he, put not on two coats.
11	And whosoever shall not receive you, nor hear you, when ye depart thence, shake off the dust under your feet	And whatsoever place shall not receive you, and they. hear you not, as ye go forth thence, shake off the dust that is under your feet
	—Verily I say unto you, It shall be more tolerable for Sodom . and Gomorrha in the day of judgment, than for that city.	omitted.

Chap.	Authorized Version.	Revised Version.
14	—therefore mighty works do shew forth themselves in him.	—therefore do these powers work in him.
15	—or as one	—even as one
16	—It is John, whom I beheaded: he is risen from the dead.	—John whom I beheaded, he is risen.
19	Therefore Herodias had a quarrel against him, and would have killed him;	And Herodias set herself against him and desired to kill him;
20	—observed him;	—kept him safe.
	—he did many things,	—he was much perplexed;
21	—chief estates	—chief men
25	—give me by and by	—forthwith give me
27	—an executioner,	—a soldier of his guard,
32	And they departed into a desert place by ship privately.	And they went away in a boat to a desert place apart.
33	—many knew him,	—many knew them,
	—and came together unto him.	} *omitted.*
34	And Jesus, when he came out, saw much people,	And he came forth and saw a great multitude,
35	—the time is far passed:	—the day is now far spent:
36	—bread:	—somewhat to eat.
	—for they have nothing to eat.	} *omitted.*
43	—twelve baskets full of the fragments,	—broken pieces, twelve basketfuls,

Chap.	Authorized Version.	Revised Version.
46	—when he had sent them away,	—after he had taken leave of them,
48	—toiling	—distressed
49	—a spirit,	—an apparition,
51	—beyond measure and wondered.	*omitted.*
52	—they considered not the miracle of the loaves:	—they understood not concerning the loaves,
53	—drew to the shore.	—moored to the shore.
54	—they knew him,	—the people knew him,
56	—streets,	—market places,
7 1	—certain of the scribes which came from Jerusalem.	—certain of the scribes, which had come from Jerusalem, and had seen that some of his disciples ate their bread with defiled, that is, unwashen, hands,
2	And when they saw some of his disciples eat bread with defiled, that is to say, with unwashen, hands,	
	—they found fault	*omitted.*
3	—oft,	—diligently,
4	—market,	—market place,
	—and of tables	*omitted.*
5	—unwashen	—defiled
7	—teaching for doctrines the commandments of men.	Teaching as their doctrines the precepts of men.
8	For laying aside the commandment of God,	Ye leave the commandment of God,

Chap.	Authorized Version.	Revised Version.
8	—as the washing of pots and cups: and many other such like things ye do.	} *omitted*.
10	—Whoso curseth father or mother,	—He that speaketh evil of father or mother,
11	But ye say, If a man shall say to his father or mother, It is Corban, that is to say, a gift, by whatsoever thou mightest be profited by me: he shall be free.	—but ye say, If a man shall say to his father or his mother, That wherewith thou mightest have been profited by me is Corban, that is to say, Given to God;
16	If any man have ears to hear, let him hear.	} *omitted*.
19	—purging all meats?	This he said, making all meats clean.
21	For from within, out of the heart of men, proceed evil thoughts, adulteries, fornications, murders,	For from within, out of the heart of men, evil thoughts proceed, fornication, thefts, murders, adulteries, covetings, wickednesses, deceit, lasciviousness, an evil eye, railing, pride, foolishness:
22	Thefts, covetousness, wickedness, deceit, lasciviousness, an evil eye, blasphemy, pride, foolishness:	
25	For a certain woman,	But straightway a woman,
	—young daughter	—little daughter
26	—nation;	—race.
33	—took him aside from the multitude,	—took him aside from the multitude privately.
35	—string	—bond

Chap.	Authorized Version.	Revised Version.
8 4	—From whence can a man satisfy these men with bread here in the wilderness?	—Whence shall one be able to fill these men with bread here in a desert place?
9	And they that had eaten were about four thousand:	And they were about four thousand:
14	Now the disciples had forgotten to take bread, neither had they in the ship with them more than one loaf.	And they forgot to take bread; and they had not in the boat with them more than one loaf.
16	—It is because we have no bread.	—We have no bread.
19	—fragments	—broken pieces
24	—I see men as trees, walking.	—I see men; for I beheld them as trees, walking.
25	—and made him look up:	—and he looked steadfastly,
26	—neither go into the town, nor tell it to any in the town.	Do not even enter into the village.
27	—towns	—villages
33	—savourest	—mindest
36	—lose his own soul?	—forfeit his life?
37	—soul?	—life?
9 3	—shining, exceeding white as snow;	—glistering, exceeding white;
6	—to say;	—to answer;
11	—Why say the scribes that Elias must first come?	—The scribes say that Elijah must first come.

Chap.	Authorized Version.	Revised Version.
12	—how it is written	—how is it written
18	—he teareth him: and he foameth, and gnasheth with his teeth,	—it dasheth him down: and he foameth, and grindeth his teeth,
19	—he answereth him,	—he answereth them,
20	—tare him;	—tare him grievously;
23	—If thou canst believe,	—If thou canst!
26	—rent him sore,	—tore him much,
	—many	—the more part
28	—Why could not we cast him out?	We could not cast it out.
29	—This kind can come forth by nothing, but by prayer and fasting.	This kind can come out by nothing, save by prayer.
33	—What was it that ye disputed among yourselves by the way?	What were ye reasoning in the way?
38	—and he followeth not us:	} *omitted.*
39	—there is no man which shall do a miracle in my name, that can lightly speak evil of me.	—there is no man which shall do a mighty work in my name, and to be able quickly to speak evil of me.
40	—on our part.	—for us.
41	—in my name,	*omitted.*
42	And whosoever shall offend one of these little ones that believe in me,	And whosoever shall cause one of these little ones that believe on me to stumble,

Chap.	Authorized Version.	Revised Version.
43	—offend thee,	—cause thee to stumble,
	—the fire that never shall be quenched.	—the unquenchable fire.
44	Where their worm dieth not, and the fire is not quenched. (*Also repetition in v.* 46.)	*omitted.*
45	—offend thee,	—cause thee to stumble,
	—into the fire that never shall be quenched :	*omitted.*
47	—offend thee	—cause thee to stumble
49	—and every sacrifice shall be salted with salt.	*omitted.*
10 1	—by the farther side of Jordan :	—and beyond Jordan
	—the people resort unto him again ;	—and multitudes come together unto him again ;
5	—precept.	—commandment
13	—rebuked those that brought them.	—rebuked them
14	—was much displeased,	—was moved with indignation,
21	—take up the cross	*omitted.*
22	—he was sad at that saying, and went away grieved :	—his countenance fell at the saying and he went away sorrowful :
26	—out of measure,	—exceedingly,
29	—or wife	*omitted.*
35	—we shall desire	—we shall ask of thee.

Chap.		Authorized Version.	Revised Version.
	41	—much displeased with James and John	—moved with indignation concerning James and John
	42	—exercise lordship over them	—lord it over them;
	44	—the chiefest,	—first among you,
	45	For even	For verily
	46	—sat by the highway side begging	—a blind beggar was sitting by the way side.
	48	—charged him	—rebuked him,
	49	—and commanded him to be called.	—and said call ye him.
	50	—rose	—sprang up.
	51	—Lord,	Rabboni.
11	3	—hither	—back hither,
	4	—in a place where two ways met;	—in the open street;
	8	—and others cut down branches off the trees and strewed them in the way	—and others branches, which they had cut from the fields
	10	Blessed be the kingdom of our father David, that cometh in the name of the Lord:	Blessed is the kingdom that cometh, the kingdom of our father David:
	13	—the time of figs was not yet.	—it was not the season of figs
	17	—My house shall be called of all nations the house of prayer?	My house shall be called a house of prayer for all the nations?
	18	—all the people was astonished at his doctrine.	—all the multitude was astonished at his teaching.

Chap.	Authorized Version.	Revised Version.
19	And when even was come he went out of the city	And every evening he went forth out of the city.
21	—Master,	—Rabbi,
23	—he shall have whatsoever he saith	—he shall have it
24	—what things soever ye desire, when ye pray,	—All things whatsoever ye pray and ask for
26	But if ye do not forgive, neither will your Father which is in heaven forgive your trespasses	} *omitted.*
32	—for all men counted John, that he was a prophet indeed	—for all verily held John to be a prophet
12 1	—a place for the winefat,	—a pit for the winepress
4	—at him they cast stones,	*omitted.*
11	—the Lord's doing,	—from the Lord
13	—to catch him in his words.	—that they might catch him in talk.
14	—but teachest the way of God in truth	—but of a truth teachest the way of God:
17	—they marvelled at him.	—they marvelled greatly at him.
23	—therefore, when they shall rise.	} *omitted.*
24	—Do ye not therefore err, because ye know not the Scriptures,	—Is it not for this cause that ye err, that ye know not the Scriptures,
26	—how in the bush God spake unto him,	—in the place concerning the Bush, how God spake unto him.

Chap.	Authorized Version.	Revised Version.
28	—reasoning	—questioning
29	—of all the commandments	omitted.
	—The Lord our God is one Lord :	—The Lord our God, the Lord is one :
30	—this is the first commandment	omitted.
31	—the second is like, namely this,	The second is this,
32	—Well, Master, thou hast said the truth : for there is one God ;	Of a truth, Master, thou hast well said that he is one ;
33	—and with all the soul	omitted.
36	—by the Holy Ghost,	—in the Holy Spirit,
	—thy footstool	—the footstool of thy feet.
38	—doctrine,	—teaching
	—love to go in long clothing,	—desire to walk in long robes,
39	—the uppermost rooms at feasts :	—chief places at feasts :
44	—abundance	—superfluity
13 1	—and what buildings are here !	—and what manner of buildings !
4	—when all these things shall be fulfilled ?	—when these things are all about to be accomplished ?
5	—deceive you :	—lead you astray
6	—deceive many	—lead many astray.
8	—and troubles	omitted.
	—these are the beginnings of sorrows.	—these things are the beginning of travail.
10	—published	—preached

Chap.	Authorized Version.	Revised Version.
11	—lead you, —take no thought —neither do ye premeditate:	—lead you to judgment, —be not anxious } *omitted.*
12	—betray	—deliver up
14	—spoken of by Daniel the prophet —where it ought not,	} *omitted.* —where he ought not,
16	—to take up his garment	—to take his cloke.
18	—And pray ye that your flight be not in the winter.	And pray ye that it be not in the winter.
19	For in those days shall be affliction, such as was not from the beginning of the creation which God created unto this time, neither shall be.	For those days shall be tribulation, such as there hath not been the like from the beginning of the creation which God created until now, and never shall be.
21	—Lo, here is Christ; or, lo, he is there;	—Lo, here is the Christ; or, Lo, there
22	—to seduce, if it were possible, even the elect.	—that they may lead astray, if possible, the elect.
25	—the stars of heaven shall fall,	—the stars shall be falling from heaven,
28	Now learn a parable of the fig tree;	Now from the fig tree learn her parable:
29	—know ye that it is nigh,	—know ye that he is nigh,
30	—done.	—accomplished.
34	For the Son of man is as a man taking a	It is as when a man, sojourning in anoth-

Chap.	Authorized Version.	Revised Version.
	far journey, who left his house, and gave authority to his servants, and to every man his work, and commanded the porter to watch.	er country, having left his house, and given authority to his servants, to each one his work, commanded also the porter to watch.
14 1	—take him by craft, and put him to death.	—take him with subtility, and kill him:
2	—lest there be an uproar	—lest haply there shall be a tumult
3	—being in Bethany	—while he was in Bethany
	—box	—cruse
4	—within themselves,	—among themselves,
	—Why was this waste of the ointment made?	—To what purpose hath this waste of the ointment been made?
10	—one of the twelve,	—he that was one of the twelve,
	—to betray him	—that he might deliver him
11	—betray him.	—deliver him unto them.
12	—killed	—sacrificed
15	—prepared:	—ready:
18	—One of you which eateth with me shall betray me.	—One of you shall betray me, even he that eateth with me.
19	—and another said, Is it I?	} *omitted.*
20	—It is one of the twelve, that dippeth with me in the dish.	—It is one of the twelve, he that dippeth with me in the dish.

Chap.	Authorized Version.	Revised Version.
22	—and blessed,	—and when he had blessed,
	—Take, eat:	—Take ye:
23	—the cup,	—a cup,
24	—the new testament,	—the covenant,
27	—because of me this night:	} omitted.
28	But after that I am risen,	Howbeit, after I am raised up,
30	—That this day, even in this night,	—that thou to-day, even this night,
31	But he spake the more vehemently, If I should die with thee, I will not deny thee in any wise. Likewise also said they all.	But he spake exceeding vehemently, If I must die with thee, I will not deny thee. And in like manner also said they all.
33	—and began to be sore amazed, and to be very heavy;	—and began to be greatly amazed, and sore troubled.
38	—ready,	—willing,
40	And when he returned, he found them asleep again,	And again he came, and found them sleeping,
42	Rise up, let us go;	Arise, let us be going:
45	—Master, master;	—Rabbi;
49	—but the scriptures must be fulfilled.	—but this is done that the scriptures might be fulfilled.
51	—the young men laid hold on him:	—and they lay hold on him;
54	—palace	—court
	—servants,	—officers,

Chap.	Authorized Version.	Revised Version.
54	—at the fire.	—in the light of the fire.
64	—guilty of death.	—worthy of death.
65	—the servants did strike him with the palms of their hands.	—the officers received him with blows of their hands.
66	—the palace,	—the court,
67	—thou also wast with Jesus of Nazareth.	—Thou also wast with the Nazarene, even Jesus.
69	And a maid saw him again, and began to say	And the maid saw him, and began again to say
70	—Surely	—Of a truth
	—and thy speech agreeth thereto.	} *omitted.*
72	And the second time	And straightway the second time
15 3	—but he answered nothing.	} *omitted.*
4	—they witness against thee.	—they accuse thee of.
5	—yet answered nothing;	—no more answered anything;
6	Now at that feast he released unto them one prisoner, whomsoever they desired.	Now at the feast he used to release unto them one prisoner, whom they asked of him.
7	—who had committed murder in the insurrection.	—men who in the insurrection had committed murder.
8	And the multitude crying aloud began to	And the multitude went up and began

Chap.	Authorized Version.	Revised Version.
	desire him to do as he had ever done unto them.	to ask him to do as he was wont to do unto them.
11	—moved the people,	—stirred up the multitude,
16	—into the hall,	—within the court,
17	—put it about his head,	—put it on him;
20	—put his own clothes on him,	—put on him his garments.
21	—Simon a Cyrenian,	—Simon of Cyrene
23	—they gave him to drink	—they offered him
28	And the scripture was fulfilled, which saith, And he was numbered with the transgressors.	*omitted*.
32	—reviled him.	—reproached him.
36	—Let alone; let us see whether Elias will come to take him down.	—Let be; let us see whether Elijah cometh to take him down.
37	—cried with a loud voice,	—uttered a loud voice,
39	—so cried out, and	*omitted*.
40	—looking on afar off:	—beholding from afar:
43	Joseph of Arimathæa, an honourable counsellor, which also waited for the kingdom of God, came, and went in boldly unto Pilate, and craved the body of Jesus.	—there came Joseph of Arimathæa, a concillor of honourable estate, who also himself was looking for the kingdom of God; and he boldly went in unto Pilate, and asked for the body of Jesus.

Chap.	Authorized Version.	Revised Version.
45	—knew it	—learned it
	—gave the body	—granted the corpse
46	—fine linen,	—a linen cloth,
	—wrapped him in the linen,	—wound him in the linen cloth,
	—sepulchre	—tomb
16 2	—very early in the morning	—very early
	—at the rising of the sun.	—when the sun was risen.
4	And when they looked, they saw that the stone was rolled away: for it was very great.	—and looking up, they see that the stone is rolled back: for it was exceeding great.
5	—clothed in a long white garment; and they were affrighted.	—arrayed in a white robe; and they were amazed.
6	—Be not affrighted:	—be not amazed:
	—Jesus of Nazareth,	—Jesus, the Nazarene,
7	But go your way	—But go,
8	And they went out quickly, and fled from the sepulchre; for they trembled and were amazed: neither said they anything to any man;	And they went out, and fled from the tomb; for trembling and astonishment had come upon them; and they said nothing to any one;
9	—when Jesus was risen	—when he was risen
12	—appeared	—was manifested
14	—he appeared unto the eleven	—he was manifested unto the eleven themselves

Chap.	Authorized Version.	Revised Version.
15	—every creature.	—the whole creation.
16	—he that believeth not shall be damned.	—he that disbelieveth shall be condèmned.
18	—it shall not hurt them;	—it shall in no wise hurt them;
19	—the Lord	—the Lord Jesus,
20	—with signs following.	—by the signs that followed.

S. LUKE.

Chap.	Authorized Version.	Revised Version.
1 1	—to set forth in order a declaration of those things which are most surely believed among us,	—to draw up a narrative concerning those matters which have been fulfilled among us,
3	—having had perfect understanding of all things from the very first,	—having traced the course of all things accurately from the first,
4	—of those things,	—concerning the things
9	—his lot was to burn incense when he went into the temple of the Lord.	—his lot was to enter into the temple of the Lord and burn incense.
10	—time	—hour
13	—prayer	—supplication
17	—go before him	—go before his face
	—to the wisdom of the just; to make ready a people prepared for the Lord.	—to walk in the wisdom of the just; to make ready for the Lord a people prepared for him.
19	—to shew thee	—to bring thee
20	—dumb,	—silent
	—be performed,	—come to pass,
21	—marvelled that he tarried so long in the temple	—marvelled while he tarried in the temple.

Chap.	Authorized Version.	Revised Version.
22	—for he beckoned unto them, and remained speechless.	—and he continued making signs unto them, and remained dumb.
23	—accomplished,	—fulfilled,
25	—dealt with me	—done unto me
27	—espoused	—betrothed
28	—blessed art thou among women.	} *omitted.*
29	—when she saw him,	*omitted.*
35	—therefore also that holy thing which shall be born of thee shall be called the Son of God.	—wherefore also that which is to be born shall be called holy, the Son of God.
36	—thy cousin Elisabeth,	—Elisabeth thy kinswoman,
37	For with God nothing shall be impossible.	For no word from God shall be void of power.
42	And she spake out with a loud voice,	—and she lifted up her voice with a loud cry,
45	—performance	—fulfilment
48	—regarded	—looked upon
50	And his mercy is on them that fear him from generation to generation.	And his mercy is unto generations and generations On them that fear him.
52	He hath put down the mighty from their seats,	He hath put down princes from their thrones,
54	—in remembrance of his mercy;	That he might remember mercy (As he spake unto our fathers) Toward Abra-
55	As he spake to our fathers, to Abraham,	

Chap.	Authorized Version.	Revised Version.
	and to his seed for ever.	ham and his seed for ever.
57	—came	—was fulfilled
58	—cousins	—kinsfolk
	—shewed great mercy upon her;	—magnified his mercy towards her;
59	—they called him	—they would have called him
64	—and praised God.	—blessing God.
66	What manner of child shall this be! And the hand of the Lord was with him.	What then shall this child be? For the hand of the Lord was with him.
68	—Lord God of Israel;	—Lord, the God of Israel;
	—redeemed his people,	—wrought redemption for his people,
71	That we should be saved from our enemies,	—Salvation from our enemies,
72	To perform the mercy promised to our fathers,	To shew mercy towards our fathers,
74	That he would grant	To grant
75	—All the days of our life.	—all our days.
76	And thou, child	Yea and thou, child
	—prepare	—make ready
77	—by the remission	In the remission
78	Through	Because of
	—hath visited us,	—shall visit us,
79	To give light to them	To shine upon them
2 1	—taxed.	—enrolled
2	(And this taxing was	This was the first en-

Chap.	Authorized Version.	Revised Version.
	first made when Cyrenius was governor of Syria)	rolment made when Quirinius was governor of Syria.
3	—to be taxed,	—to enrol themselves,
4	—lineage	—family
5	To be taxed with Mary his espoused wife,	—to enrol himself with Mary, who was betrothed to him,
6	And so it was, that, —accomplished	And it came to pass, —fulfilled
9	—came upon them,	—stood by them,
14	—and on earth peace, good will toward men.	And on earth peace among men in whom he is well pleased.
17	—which was told them concerning this child.	—which was spoken to them about this child.
22	—her purification	—their purification
25	—and the same man was just	—and this man was righteous
28	—took he him up in his arms,	—received him into his arms,
29	Lord, now lettest thou thy servant depart in peace, according to thy word:	Now lettest thou thy servant depart, O Lord, According to thy word, in peace;
31	—all people;	—all peoples;
32	A light to lighten the Gentiles,	A light for revelation to the Gentiles,
33	And Joseph —of him.	And his father —concerning him;
34	—rising again —which shall be	—rising up —which is

Chap.	Authorized Version.	Revised Version.
35	—the thoughts of many hearts	—thoughts out of many hearts
37	—she was a widow of about	—she had been a widow even for
	—but served God with fastings and prayers	—worshipping with fastings and supplications
38	And she coming in that instant gave thanks likewise unto the Lord,	And coming up at that very hour she gave thanks unto God,
39	—performed	—accomplished
40	—strong in spirit,	—strong,
42	—they went up to Jerusalem	—they went up
43	—child Jesus	—boy Jesus
	—Joseph and his mother knew not of it.	—his parents knew it not;
47	—astonished	—amazed
49	—about my Father's business?	—in my Father's house?
52	—increased	—advanced
3 1	—Ituræa and the region of Trachonitis,	—the region of Ituræa and Trachonitis,
2	Annas and Caiaphas being the high priests,	—in the high-priesthood of Annas and Caiaphas,
4	—Prepare	—Make ye ready
7	Then said he	He said therefore
	—O generation of vipers,	—Ye offspring of vipers,
10	—the people	—the multitudes
11	—meat	—food,
12	—what shall we do?	—what must we do?

Chap.	Authorized Version.	Revised Version.
13	—Exact	—Extort
14	—demanded of him,	—asked him,
	—neither accuse any falsely;	—neither exact anything wrongfully;
15	—and all men mused in their hearts of John, whether he were the Christ, or not;	—and all men reasoned in their hearts concerning John, whether haply he were the Christ;
17	—and he will throughly purge his floor,	—throughly to cleanse his threshing-floor,
18	And many other things in his exhortation preached he unto the people.	With many other exhortations therefore preached he good tidings unto the people;
21	—being baptized,	—having been baptized,
22	—which said,	*omitted.*
23	And Jesus himself began to be about thirty years of age,	And Jesus himself . when he began to teach, was about thirty years of age,
4 1	—Holy Ghost	—Holy Spirit,
	—was led by the Spirit into the wilderness,	—was led by the Spirit in the wilderness
2	Being forty days tempted of the devil.	during forty days, being tempted of the devil.
	—when they were ended, he afterward hungered.	—when they were completed, he hungered.
4	—but by every word of God.	} *omitted.*
5	And the devil, taking him up	And he led him up

Chap.	Authorized Version.	Revised Version.
5	—into an high mountain	*omitted.*
6	—All this power will I give thee,	To thee will I give all this authority,
8	—Get thee behind me, Satan : for	*omitted.*
10	—charge over thee, to keep thee:	—charge concerning thee, to guard thee :
11	—lest at any time thou dash	Lest haply thou dash
13	—ended all the temptation,	—completed every temptation,
18	—the gospel	—good tidings
	—he hath sent me to heal the brokenhearted, to preach deliverance to the captives, and recovering of sight to the blind, to set at liberty them that are bruised,	He hath sent me to proclaim release to the captives, And recovering of sight to the blind, To set at liberty them that are bruised,
19	To preach the acceptable year of the Lord.	To proclaim the acceptable year of the Lord.
20	—gave it again to the minister,	—gave it back to the attendant,
22	—gracious words	—words of grace
23	—Ye will surely say unto me this proverb,	—Doubtless ye will say unto me this parable,
24	—accepted	—acceptable
26	—Sarepta, a city of Sidon,	Zarephath, in the land of Sidon,
27	—saving	—but only
28	And all they in the synagogue, when	And they were all filled with wrath in the

Chap.	Authorized Version.	Revised Version.
	they heard these things, were filled with wrath,	synagogue, as they heard these things;
31	—And taught them	And he was teaching them
32	—doctrine:	—teaching;
	—power.	—authority.
34	Saying, Let us alone; what have we to do with thee,	Ah! what have we to do with thee,
35	—and hurt him not.	—having done him no hurt.
36	And they were all amazed, and spake among themselves, saying, What a word is this!	And amazement came upon them all, and they spake together, one with another, saying, What is this word?
37	And the fame of him went out into every place of the country round about.	And there went forth a rumour concerning him into every place of the region round about.
38	—taken	—holden
41	—Thou art Christ the Son of God.	—Thou art the Son of God.
42	—the people sought him,	—the multitudes sought after him,
43	—the kingdom of God	—the good tidings of the kingdom of God
5 3	—prayed him that he would thrust out	—asked him to put out
	—the people	—the multitudes
4	—Launch out	—Put out

Chap.	Authorized Version.	Revised Version.
6	—their net brake.	—their nets were breaking;
9	—astonished,	—amazed,
15	—went there a fame abroad of him:	—went abroad the report concerning him:
16	—into the wilderness,	—in the deserts,
17	—on a certain day,	—on one of those days,
	—was present to heal them,	—was with him to heal.
18	—taken with a palsy:	—that was palsied:
22	—perceived their thoughts,	—perceiving their reasonings,
26	And they were all amazed,	And amazement took hold on all,
27	—receipt of custom:	—place of toll,
30	But their scribes and Pharisees	And the Pharisees and their scribes
33	—Why do the disciples of John fast often, and make prayers, and likewise the disciples of the Pharisees; but thine eat and drink?	The disciples of John fast often, and make supplications; likewise also the disciples of the Pharisees; but thine eat and drink.
34	—children	—sons
36	—No man putteth a piece of a new garment upon an old; if otherwise, then both the new maketh a rent, and the piece that was taken out of the new agreeth not with the old.	—No man rendeth a piece from a new garment and putteth it upon an old garment; else he will rend the new, and also the piece from the new will not agree with the old.
37	—old bottles;	—old wine-skins;

Chap.	Authorized Version.	Revised Version.
37	—bottles,	—skins,
38	—new bottles;	—fresh wine-skins.
	—and both are preserved.	} omitted.
39	—better.	—good.
6 1	—on the second sabbath after the first,	—on a sabbath,
3	—so much as this,	—even this,
5	—Lord also of the sabbath.	—lord of the sabbath.
7	—an accusation against him.	—how to accuse him.
9	—evil?	—harm?
10	—whole as the other.	*omitted.*
15	—Zelotes,	—the Zealot,
16	—Judas the brother of James,	—Judas the son of James
17	—in the plain,	—on a level place,
	—and the company of his disciples, and a great multitude of people	—and a great multitude of his disciples, and a great number of people
18	And they that were vexed with unclean spirits: and they were healed.	—and they that were troubled with unclean spirits were healed.
19	—for there went virtue out of him,	—for power came forth from him,
26	—for so	—for in the same manner
29	—forbid not to take thy coat also.	—withhold not thy coat also.
34	—to receive as much again	—to receive again as much

Chap.	Authorized Version.	Revised Version.
35	—hoping for nothing again;	—never despairing;
37	—forgive, and ye shall be forgiven:	—release, and ye shall be released:
39	—the ditch?	—a pit?
40	—that is perfect	—when his is perfected
41	—perceivest	—considerest
43	For a good tree bringeth not forth corrupt fruit; neither doth a corrupt tree bring forth good fruit.	For there is no good tree that bringeth forth corrupt fruit; nor again a corrupt tree that bringeth forth good fruit.
47	Whosoever cometh to me, and heareth my sayings,	Every one that cometh unto me, and heareth my words,
48	—which built an house, and digged deep	—building a house, who digged and went deep.
	—beat vehemently upon	—brake against
	—for it was founded upon a rock.	—because it had been well builded.
49	—did beat vehemently, and immediately it fell;	—brake, and straightway it fell in;
7 1	Now when he had ended all his sayings in the audience of the people,	After he had ended all his sayings in the ears of the people,
2	—ready to die.	—at the point of death.
3	—beseeching him that he would come and heal his servant.	—asking him that he would come and save his servant.
4	—instantly,	—earnestly,

Chap.	Authorized Version.	Revised Version.
	—That he was worthy for whom he should do this:	—He is worthy that thou shouldest do this for him:
5	—and he hath built us a synagogue.	—and himself built us our synagogue.
9	—people	—multitude
10	—that had been sick.	*omitted.*
11	—the day after,	—soon afterwards,
	—and many of his disciples went with him, and much people.	—and his disciples went with him, and a great multitude.
14	—they that bare him	—the bearers
15	—delivered him	—gave him
16	—there came a fear on all:	—fear took hold on all:
17	—rumour	—report
18	—shewed him	—told him
19	—Jesus,	—the Lord,
20	—John Baptist	—John the Baptist
21	—infirmities	—diseases
	—gave sight.	—bestowed sight.
22	—to the poor the gospel is preached.	—the poor have good tidings preached to them.
23	—whosoever shall not be offended in me.	—whosoever shall find none occasion of stumbling in me.
24	—began to speak unto the people concerning John,	—began to say unto the multitudes concerning John,
	—to see?	—to behold?
28	—John the Baptist:	—John:
	—he that is least	—he that is but little

Chap.	Authorized Version.	Revised Version.
30	—rejected the counsel of God against themselves,	—rejected for themselves the counsel of God,
31	And the Lord said,	*omitted.*
32	—we have mourned to you,	—we wailed,
37	—box	—cruse
39	—known	—perceived
41	There was a certain creditor which	A certain lender
42	And when they had nothing to pay, he frankly forgave them both. Tell me therefore, which of them will love him most?	When they had not wherewith to pay, he forgave them both. Which of them therefore will love him most?
44	—she hath washed my feet with tears, and wiped them with the hairs of her head.	—she hath wetted my feet with her tears, and wiped them with her hair.
49	—that forgiveth sins also?	—that even forgiveth sins?
8 1	—he went throughout every city and village,	—he went about through cities and villages,
	—shewing	—bringing
3	—ministered unto him	—ministered unto them
4	—when much people were gathered together, and were come to him out of every city,	—when a great multitude came together, and they of every city resorted unto him,
5	—trodden down,	—trodden under foot,
	—fowls of the air	—birds of the heaven

Chap.	Authorized Version.	Revised Version.
8	—when he had said these things,	As he said these things,
14	—go forth,	—and as they go on their way
15	—keep it,	—hold it fast,
16	—candle, —candlestick,	—lamp, —stand,
17	—secret, —hid, —come abroad.	—hid, —secret, —come to light.
18	—seemeth to have.	—thinketh he hath.
19	—press.	—crowd.
20	—by certain which said,	*omitted*.
23	—filled with water,	—filling with water,
25	—And they being afraid wondered, What manner of man is this!	And being afraid they marvelled, Who then is this,
26	—Gadarenes,	—Gerasenes,
27	—which had devils long time, and ware no clothes,	—who had devils; and for a long time he had worn no clothes,
29	—he was kept bound —wilderness.	—he was kept under guard, and bound —deserts.
31	—besought —the deep.	—intreated —the abyss.
32	—suffer them —he suffered them.	—give them leave —he gave them leave.
33	—a steep place	—the steep
34	—what was done,	—what had come to pass,
36	—by what means	—how

Chap.	Authorized Version.	Revised Version.
37	—the whole multitude	—all the people
	—taken	—holden
	—returned back again.	—returned.
40	—it came to pass,	*omitted*.
	—the people gladly received him :	—the multitude welcomed him ;
45	—the multitude throng thee and press thee,	—the multitudes press thee and crush thee.
	—and sayest thou, Who touched me?	} *omitted*.
46	—virtue is gone out of me.	—power had gone forth from me.
48	—be of good comfort :	*omitted*.
54	And he put them all out,	} *omitted*.
55	—to give her meat.	—that something be given her to eat.
56	—astonished :	—amazed :
9 1	—his twelve disciples	—the twelve
3	—neither staves, nor scrip,	—neither staff, nor wallet,
	—two coats apiece.	—two coats.
6	—towns,	—villages,
9	—desired	—sought
10	—and went aside privately into a desert place belonging to the city called Bethsaida.	—and withdrew apart to a city called Bethsaida.
11	And the people, when they knew it,	But the multitudes perceiving it
	—received them,	—welcomed them,

Chap.	Authorized Version.	Revised Version.
14	—by fifties in a company.	—in companies, about fifty each.
17	—of fragments that remained to them	—that which remained over to them of broken pieces,
25	—advantaged,	—profited,
	—and lose himself, or be cast away?	—and lose or forfeit his own self?
29	—was white and glistering.	—became white and dazzling.
31	—should accomplish	—was about to accomplish
32	—awake,	—fully awake,
35	—This is my beloved Son: hear him.	—This is my Son, my chosen: hear ye him.
36	—was past,	—came,
	—kept it close,	—held their peace,
39	—and bruising him hardly departeth from him.	—and it hardly departeth from him, bruising him sorely.
41	—and suffer you?	—and bear with you?
42	—the devil threw him down, and tare him.	—the devil dashed him down, and tare him grievously.
43	—amazed at the mighty power of God.	—astonished at the majesty of God.
45	—hid	—concealed
47	—thought	—reasoning
	—by him,	—by his side,
50	—us.	—you.
51	—the time was come	—the days were well-nigh come
53	—would go	—were going

Chap.	Authorized Version.	Revised Version.
54	—command	—bid
	—even as Elias did?	*omitted.*
55	—and said, Ye know not what manner of spirit ye are of.	*omitted.*
56	For the Son of man is not come to destroy men's lives, but to save them.	*omitted.*
57	—it came to pass,	*omitted.*
60	—Let the dead bury their dead:	Leave the dead to bury their own dead;
	—preach	—publish abroad
10 2	—truly is great,	—is plenteous,
4	Carry neither purse, nor scrip, nor shoes:	Carry no purse, no wallet, no shoes:
11	—notwithstanding be ye sure of this, that the kingdom of God is come nigh unto you.	—howbeit know this, that the kingdom of God is come nigh.
15	And thou, Capernaum, which art exalted to heaven, shall be thrust down to hell.	And thou Capernaum, shalt thou be exalted unto heaven? thou shalt be brought down unto Hades.
16	—despiseth	—rejecteth
21	—prudent,	—understanding,
	—for so it seemed good	—for so it was well-pleasing
22	—will reveal him.	—willeth to reveal him.
29	—willing	—desiring
30	—which stripped him of his raiment, and wounded him,	—which both stripped him and beat him,

Chap.		Authorized Version.	Revised Version.
	32	—when he was at the place, came and looked on him,	—when he came to the place, and saw him,
	33	—had compassion on him,	—was moved with compassion,
	34	—pouring in	—pouring on them
	35	—when he departed,	*omitted.*
	36	—was neighbour unto him that fell among the thieves?	—proved neighbour unto him that fell among the robbers?
	38	Now it came to pass as they went,	Now as they went on their way,
	39	—Jesus' feet,	—the Lord's feet,
	41	—careful	—anxious
11	2	—Our Father	—Father,
		—which art in heaven,	*omitted.*
		—Thy will be done, as in heaven, so in earth.	} *omitted.*
	4	—for we also forgive	—for we ourselves also forgive
		—And lead us not	And bring us not
		—but deliver us from evil.	} *omitted.*
	6	—in his journey is come to me,	—is come to me from a journey,
	11	If a son shall ask bread of any of you that is a father,	And which of you that is a father shall his son ask a loaf,
	14	—the dumb spake;	—the dumb man spake;
		—wondered.	—marvelled.
	15	—chief	—prince
	21	—keepeth his palace,	—guardeth his own court,

Chap.	Authorized Version.	Revised Version.
24	—dry places,	—waterless places,
27	—of the company	—out of the multitude
29	—gathered thick together,	—gathering together unto him,
	—the prophet.	*omitted.*
31	—utmost parts of the earth	—ends of the earth
33	—candle	—lamp,
	—a secret place,	—a cellar,
	—a candlestick,	—the stand,
34	—light	—lamp
	—when thine eye is evil,	—when it is evil,
35	Take heed therefore that	Look therefore whether
36	—as when the bright shining of a candle	—as when the lamp with its bright shining
39	—ravening	—extortion
40	—fools,	—foolish ones,
41	But rather give alms of such things as ye have;	Howbeit give for alms those things which are within;
42	—all manner of herbs,	—every herb,
43	—uppermost	—chief
	—greetings in the markets.	—salutations in the market places.
44	—scribes and Pharisees, hypocrites!	} *omitted.*
	—are not aware of them.	—know it not.
48	Truly ye bear witness that ye allow the deeds of your fathers: for they in-	So ye are witnesses and consent unto the works of your fathers: for they kill-

Chap.	Authorized Version.	Revised Version.
	deed killed them, and ye build their sepulchres.	ed them, and ye build their tombs.
51	—temple:	—sanctuary:
53	And as he said these things unto them,	And when he was come out from thence,
	—urge him	—press upon him
54	—that they might accuse him.	} *omitted.*
12 1	—an innumerable multitude of people,	—the many thousands of the multitude
3	—closets	—inner chambers
10	—Holy Ghost	—Holy Spirit
11	—and unto magistrates, and powers, take no thought	—and the rulers, and the authorities, be not anxious
13	—one of the company	—one out of the multitude
15	—beware of covetousness:	—keep yourselves from all covetousness:
17	—thought	—reasoned
18	—fruits	—corn
20	—Thou fool,	—Thou foolish one,
22	—Take no thought	—Be not anxious
24	—storehouse	—storechamber
	—how much more are ye better than the fowls?	—of how much more value are ye than the birds!
25	—with taking thought	—by being anxious
26	—why take ye thought	—why are ye anxious
31	But rather seek ye the kingdom of God;	Howbeit seek ye his kingdom,

Chap.	Authorized Version.	Revised Version.
33	—provide yourselves bags	—make for yourselves purses
	—approacheth,	—draweth near,
	—corrupteth.	—destroyeth.
35	—lights	—lamps
36	—wedding;	—marriage feast;
39	—goodman	—master
42	—shall make ruler over	—shall set over
45	—maidens,	—maidservants,
46	—when he looketh not for him,	—when he expecteth not,
	—is not aware,	—knoweth not,
	—unbelievers.	—unfaithful.
47	—prepared not himself,	—made not ready,
55	—heat;	—a scorching heat;
56	—discern	—interpret
59	—thou shalt not depart thence,	Thou shalt by no means come out thence,
13 4	—sinners	—offenders
7	—dresser of his vineyard,	—vinedresser,
14	—sabbath day.	—day of the sabbath.
15	—Thou hypocrite,	—Ye hypocrites,
17	—ashamed:	—put to shame:
19	—waxed	—became
	—fowls of the air	—birds of the heaven
24	—the strait gate:	—the narrow door:
31	The same day	In that very hour
	—will kill thee.	—would fain kill thee.
33	—I must walk to day,	—I must go on my way
35	—the time come when	*omitted*.

Chap.	Authorized Version.	Revised Version.
14 1	—one of the chief Pharisees	—one of the rulers of the Pharisees
5	—pit,	—well,
7	—rooms;	—seats;
8	—wedding,	—marriage feast,
	—highest room;	—chief seat;
9	—lowest room.	—lowest place.
10	—worship	—glory
11	—abased;	—humbled;
14	—for they cannot recompense thee:	—because they have not wherewith to recompense thee:
18	—a piece of ground,	—a field,
21	—halt,	—lame.
23	—compel	—constrain
28	—intending	—desiring
	—sufficient to finish it?	—wherewith to complete it?
31	—going to make war against another king, sitteth not down first, and consulteth	—as he goeth to encounter another king in war, will not sit down first and take counsel
32	—desireth	—asketh
33	—forsaketh	—renounceth
34	Salt is good: but if the salt	Salt therefore is good: but if even the salt
15 7	—likewise joy shall be in heaven	—even so there shall be joy in heaven
8	—candle,	—lamp,
10	Likewise,	Even so,
12	—goods	—thy substance

Chap.		Authorized Version.	Revised Version.
	16	—filled his belly	—been filled
	18	—before thee,	—in thy sight :
	20	—had compassion	—was moved with compassion,
	22	—Bring forth	—Bring forth quickly
	23	—be merry :	—make merry :
	26	—meant.	—might be.
	29	—neither transgressed I at any time thy commandment :	—and I never transgressed a commandment of thine :
16	1	—had wasted	—was wasting,
	3	—I cannot dig ;	I have not strength to dig ;
	5	So he called every one of his lord's debtors unto him,	And calling to him each one of his lord's debtors,
	6	—bill, (*Also in v. 7.*)	—bond,
	8	—unjust	—unrighteous
		—for the children of this world are in their generation wiser than the children of light.	—for the sons of this world are for their own generation wiser than the sons of light.
	9	—Make to yourselves friends of the mammon of unrighteousness ; that, when ye fail, they may receive you into everlasting habitations.	—Make to yourselves friends by means of the mammon of unrighteousness ; that, when it shall fail, they may receive you into the eternal tabernacles.
	10	—in that which is least	—in a very little
		—unjust	—unrighteous

Chap.	Authorized Version.	Revised Version.
10	—in the least	—in a very little
14	—covetous, —derided him.	—lovers of money, —scoffed at him.
15	—highly esteemed	—exalted
16	—since that time the kingdom of God is preached, and every man presseth into it.	—from that time the gospel of the kingdom of God is preached, and every man entereth violently into it.
23	—hell	—Hades
24	—I am tormented	—I am in anguish
25	—but now he is comforted, and thou art tormented.	—but now here he is comforted, and thou art in anguish.
26	—so that they which would pass from hence to you cannot; neither can they pass to us, that would come from thence.	—that they which would pass from hence to you may not be able, and that none may cross over from thence to us.
17 1	—offences	—occasions of stumbling
2	—than that he should offend one of these little ones.	—rather than that he should cause one of these little ones to stumble.
3	—trespass against thee,	—sin,
4	—trespass	—sin
6	—ye might say —Be thou plucked up by the root, —and it should obey you.	—ye would say —Be thou rooted up, —and it would have obeyed you.

Chap.	Authorized Version.	Revised Version.
7	But which of you, having a servant plowing or feeding cattle, will say unto him by and by, when he is come from the field, Go and sit down to meat?	But who is there of you, having a servant plowing or keeping sheep, that will say unto him, when he is come in from the field, Come straightway and sit down to meat;
9	—I trow not.	*omitted*.
11	—as he went to Jerusalem,	—as they were on the way to Jerusalem,
18	There are not found that returned to give glory to God, save this stranger.	Were there none found that returned to give glory to God, save this stranger?
20	—when he was demanded of the Pharisees,	And being asked by the Pharisees,
23	—See here; or, see there: go not after them nor follow them.	Lo, there! Lo, here! go not away, nor follow after them.
27	—they married wives,	—they married,
28	Likewise also as it was in the days of Lot;	Likewise even as it came to pass in the days of Lot;
30	Even thus	—after the same manner
31	—stuff	—goods
33	—save	—gain
18 3	—came unto him,	—came oft unto him,
5	—lest by her continual coming she weary me.	—lest she wear me out by her continual coming.
6	—unjust	—unrighteous

Chap.	Authorized Version.	Revised Version.
7	—though he bear long with them?	—and he is longsuffering over them?
9	—and despised others:	—and set all others at nought:
11	—as other men are,	—as the rest of men,
12	—possess.	—get.
14	—abased:	—humbled;
15	—infants,	—their babes,
19	—that is, God.	—even God.
21	—All these have I kept	All these things have I observed
24	And when Jesus saw that he was very sorrowful, he said,	And Jesus seeing him said,
28	—left all,	—left our own,
29	—or parents, or brethren, or wife,	—or wife, or brethren, or parents
30	—life everlasting.	—eternal life.
31	—concerning the Son of man shall be accomplished.	—shall be accomplished unto the Son of man.
32	—spitefully entreated, and spitted on:	—shamefully entreated, and spit upon:
33	—put him to death:	—kill him:
34	—neither knew they	—they perceived not
39	—cried so much the more,	—cried out the more a great deal,
42	—saved thee.	—made thee whole.
19 1	—passed through Jericho.	—was passing through Jericho.
2	—chief among the publicans,	—a chief publican,

Chap.	Authorized Version.	Revised Version.
3	—the press,	—the crowd,
7	—he was gone to be guest	He is gone in to lodge
8	—if I have taken any thing from any man by false accusation,	—if I have wrongfully exacted aught of any man,
11	—thought	—supposed
13	—Occupy till I come.	—Trade ye herewith till I come.
14	—message	—ambassage
15	—returned,	—come back again,
16	—hath gained ten pounds.	—hath made ten pounds more.
23	—that at my coming I might have required mine own with usury?	—and I at my coming should have required it with interest?
28	—ascending	—going
37	—come nigh,	—now drawing nigh,
40	—the stones would immediately cry out.	—the stones will cry out.
42	—If thou hadst known, even thou, at least in this thy day, the things which belong unto thy peace!	If thou hadst known in this day, even thou, the things which belong unto peace!
43	—trench	—bank
44	—lay thee even with the ground,	—dash thee to the ground,
45	—and them that bought;	*omitted.*
47	—chief	—principal men
48	—were very attentive to hear him.	—all hung upon him, listening.

Chap.	Authorized Version.	Revised Version.
20 3	—I will also ask you one thing; and answer me:	I also will ask you a question; and tell me:
7	—they could not tell	—they knew not
9	—a far country	—another country
11	—entreated	—handled
12	And again he sent a third:	And he sent yet a third:
13	—when they see him.	*omitted.*
14	—among themselves,	—one with another,
17	—is become	—was made
18	—broken;	—broken to pieces;
	—it will grind him to powder.	—it will scatter him as dust.
20	—which should feign themselves just men,	—which feigned themselves to be righteous,
	—words,	—speech,
	—power	—rule
23	—Why tempt ye me?	*omitted.*
26	—his words	—the saying
34	—children (*Also in v. 36*).	—sons
37	—at the bush,	—in the place concerning the Bush,
43	—thy footstool.	—the footstool of thy feet.
45	—audience	—hearing
46	—greetings in the markets,	—salutations in the market places,
46	—rooms	—places
47	—damnation.	—condemnation.

Chap.		Authorized Version.	Revised Version.
21	4	—of their abundance cast in unto the offerings of God:	—of their superfluity cast in unto the gifts:
		—penury	—want
	5	—gifts,	—offerings,
	7	—shall come to pass?	—are about to come to pass?
	8	—deceived:	—led astray:
		—I am Christ;	—I am he;
		—the time draweth near:	—The time is at hand:
	9	—commotions,	—tumults,
		—by and by.	—immediately.
	11	—fearful sights	—terrors
	12	—being brought before kings and rulers	—bringing you before kings and governors
	15	—to gainsay nor resist.	—to withstand or to gainsay.
	16	—betrayed	—delivered up
	19	—possess ye your souls.	—ye shall win your souls.
	20	—the desolation thereof is nigh.	—her desolation is at hand.
	25	—and upon the earth distress of nations, with perplexity; the sea and the waves roaring;	—and upon the earth distress of nations, in perplexity for the roaring of the sea and the billows;
	26	Men's hearts failing them for fear, and for looking after those things which are coming on the earth:	—men fainting for fear, and for expectation of the things which are coming on the world:
	30	—is now nigh at hand.	—is now nigh.
	32	—fulfilled.	—accomplished.

Chap.		Authorized Version.	Revised Version.
	34	—unawares.	—suddenly as a snare:
	35	For as a snare	—for so
	36	Watch ye therefore, and pray always, that ye may be accounted worthy to escape	But watch ye at every season, making supplication, that ye may prevail to escape
	37	And in the day time —and at night	And every day —and every night
22	2	—kill him;	—put him to death;
	3	—surnamed	—who was called
	4	—betray	—deliver
	6	—promised,	—consented,
	7	—killed	—sacrificed.
	8	—prepare us	—make ready for us
	9	—prepare?	—make ready?
	10	—where he entereth in.	—whereinto he goeth.
	14	—the twelve apostles	—the apostles
	16	—I will not any more eat thereof,	—I will not eat it,
	17	—took the cup,	—received a cup,
	20	—This cup is the new testament in my blood, which is shed for you.	—This cup is the new covenant in my blood, even that which is poured out for you.
	23	—enquire	—question
	24	And there was also a strife among them, which of them should be accounted the greatest.	And there arose also a contention among them, which of them is accounted to be greatest.
	25	—exercise	—have

Chap.	Authorized Version.	Revised Version.
27	—among you	—in the midst of you
31	And the Lord said,	*omitted.*
32	But I have prayed for thee, that thy faith fail not: and when thou art converted, strengthen thy brethren.	—but I made supplication for thee, that thy faith fail not: and do thou, when once thou hast turned again, stablish thy brethren.
35	—scrip, *(Also in v. 36).*	—wallet,
36	—and he that hath no sword, let him sell his garment, and buy one.	—and he that hath none, let him sell his cloke, and buy a sword.
37	—accomplished	—fulfilled
	—for the things concerning me have an end.	—for that which concerneth me hath fulfilment.
39	—as he was wont,	—as his custom was,
41	—withdrawn	—parted
44	—was	—became
52	—come to him,	—come against him,
54	—took	—seized
55	—hall,	—court,
56	—by the fire,	—in the light of the fire,
59	—fellow	—man
61	—Before the cock crow,	—Before the cock crow this day,
64	—they struck him on the face,	} *omitted.*
65	And many other things blasphemously spake they against him.	And many other things spake they against him, reviling him.

Chap.	Authorized Version.	Revised Version.
66	—the elders of the people and the chief priests and the scribes came together,	—the assembly of the elders of the people was gathered together, both chief priests and scribes;
67	Art thou the Christ? tell us.	If thou art the Christ, tell us.
68	—nor let me go.	*omitted.*
69	Hereafter shall the Son of man sit on the right hand of the power of God.	But from henceforth shall the Son of man be seated at the right hand of the power of God.
23 1	—multitude	—company
4	—the people,	—the multitudes,
5	—fierce,	—urgent,
	—Jewry,	—Judæa,
6	—of Galilee,	—it,
7	—at that time.	—in these days.
8	—he had heard many things of him;	—he had heard concerning him;
11	—men of war	—soldiers
	—robe,	—apparel
15	—for I sent you to him;	—for he sent him back unto us;
	—is done unto him.	—hath been done by him.
17	For of necessity he must release one unto them at the feast.	*omitted.*
18	—all at once,	—all together,
20	—willing	—desiring

Chap.	Authorized Version.	Revised Version.
23	—And the voices of them and of the chief priests prevailed.	—And their voices prevailed.
24	—that it should be as they required.	—that what they asked for should be done.
25	—sedition	—insurrection
32	—other,	—others,
33	—Calvary,	—The skull,
35	—derided him,	—scoffed at him,
	—if he be Christ, the chosen of God.	—if this is the Christ of God, his chosen.
39	—If thou be Christ,	—Art not thou the Christ?
42	—into thy kingdom.	—in thy kingdom.
44	—all the earth	—the whole land
45	—the sun was darkened,	—the sun's light failing:
48	—people	—multitudes
50	—just:	—righteous
51	—waited for	—was looking for
52	—begged	—asked for
53	—sepulchre	—tomb
24 1	—very early in the morning,	—at early dawn,
4	—shining garments:	—dazzling apparel:
10	It was Mary Magdalene, and Joanna, and Mary the mother of James, and other women that were with them, which told these things unto the apostles.	Now they were Mary Magdalene, and Joanna, and Mary the mother of James: and the other women with them told these things unto the apostles.

Chap.	Authorized Version.	Revised Version.
11	—seemed to them	—appeared in their sight
14	—they talked together	—they communed with each other
15	—reasoned,	—questioned
17	—What manner of communications are these that ye have one to another, as ye walk, and are sad?	What communications are these that ye have one with another, as ye walk? And they stood still, looking sad.
18	—Art thou only a stranger in Jerusalem,	Dost thou alone sojourn in Jerusalem
22	—made us astonished, which were early at the sepulchre;	—amazed us, having been early at the tomb;
26	Ought not Christ	Behoved it not the Christ
27	—expounded	—interpreted
35	And they told what things were done in the way,	And they rehearsed the things that happened in the way,
38	—why do thoughts arise in your hearts?	—wherefore do reasonings arise in your heart?
39	—as ye see me have.	—as ye behold me having.
42	—and of an honeycomb.	*omitted.*
46	—Thus it is written, and thus it behoved Christ to suffer,	Thus it is written, that the Christ should suffer,
49	—in the city of Jerusalem,	—in the city,
	—endued	—clothed

Chap.	Authorized Version.	Revised Version.
50	—as far as Bethany,	—until they were over against Bethany:
53	—were continually in the temple, praising and blessing God. Amen.	—were continually in the temple, blessing God.

S. JOHN.

Chap.	Authorized Version.	Revised Version.
1 5	—comprehended	—apprehended
6	There was a man	There came a man
8	—but was sent to bear witness	—but came that he might bear witness
9	That was the true Light, which lighteth every man that cometh into the world.	There was the true light, even the light which lighteth every man coming into the world.
11	—his own	—they that were his own
12	—power	—the right
	—sons of God,	—children of God,
15	—is preferred before me:	—is become before me:
19	—record	—witness
21	—that prophet? (*Also in v.* 25).	—the prophet?
24	And they which were sent were of the Pharisees.	And they had been sent from the Pharisees.
27	—is preferred before me,	*omitted*.
28	—in Bethabara	—in Bethany
29	The next day	On the morrow
30	—is preferred before me:	—is become before me
31	—therefore am I come	—for this cause came I
32	—record,	—witness,
	—I saw	—I have beheld

Chap.	Authorized Version.	Revised Version.
33	—remaining	—abiding
34	—I saw and bare record	—I have seen, and have borne witness
35	—the next day after	—on the morrow
38	—dwellest	—abidest
41	—the Christ.	—Christ.
42	—Iona:	—John:
	—A stone.	—Peter.
43	The day following Jesus would go forth into Galilee,	On the morrow he was minded to go forth into Galilee,
2 2	—called,	—bidden,
3	—when they wanted wine,	—when the wine failed,
8	—governor	—ruler
9	—that was made wine,	—now become wine,
10	—at the beginning doth set forth	—setteth on first
	—well drunk,	—drunk freely,
11	—of miracles	—of his signs
12	—and they continued there	—and there they abode
15	—drove them all out	—cast all out
23	—the miracles	—his signs
24	—commit himself	—trust himself
25	—testify of man:	—bear witness concerning man;
3 2	—these miracles	—these signs
3	—again, (*Also in v.* 7).	—anew,
10	—a master	—the teacher

Chap.	Authorized Version.	Revised Version.
10	—knowest	—understandest
11	—testify	—bear witness
13	—came down from	—descended out of
16	—everlasting	—eternal
17	—condemn	—judge
18	—condemned :	—judged :
19	—condemnation,	—judgment,
20	—evil	—ill
	—deeds	—works
32	—testifieth ;	—beareth witness ;
	—testimony.	—witness.
33	—hath set to his seal	—hath set his seal to this,
34	—giveth not the Spirit by measure unto him.	—giveth not the Spirit by measure.
36	—believeth not the Son	—obeyeth not the Son
4 12	—children,	—sons,
14	—be in him	—become in him
15	—come hither	—come all the way hither
18	—in that saidst thou truly.	—this hast thou said truly.
23	—for the Father seeketh such to worship him.	—for such doth the Father seek to be his worshippers.
29	—is not this the Christ ?	—can this be the Christ ?
31	—Master,	—Rabbi,
34	—finish	—accomplish
39	—for the saying	—because of the word
42	—the Christ,	*omitted.*

Chap.	Authorized Version.	Revised Version.
43	—he departed thence, and went into Galilee.	—he went forth from thence into Galilee.
48	—ye will not believe.	—ye will in no wise believe.
54	—miracle	—sign
5 2	—sheep market	—sheep gate
3	—a great multitude of impotent folk,	—a multitude of them that were sick,
	—waiting for the moving of the water.	
4	For an angel went down at a certain season into the pool, and troubled the water: whosoever then first after the troubling of the water stepped in was made whole of whatsoever disease he had.	*omitted.*
7	The impotent man	The sick man
14	—come upon thee.	—befall thee.
16	—therefore	—for this cause
17	—hitherto,	—even until now,
24	—condemnation;	—judgment,
29	—evil,	—ill,
	—damnation.	—judgment.
30	—just;	—righteous;
35	He was a burning and a shining light:	He was the lamp that burneth and shineth:
36	—finish,	—accomplish,

Chap.	Authorized Version.	Revised Version.
39	Search the scriptures; for in them ye think ye have eternal life: and they are they which testify of me.	Ye search the scriptures, because ye think that in them ye have eternal life; and these are they which bear witness of me;
41	—honour (*Also in v.* 44).	—glory
42	—in you.	—in yourselves.
45	—in whom ye trust.	—on whom ye have set your hope.
6 1	—over the sea	—away to the other side of the sea
2	—miracles	—signs
	—diseased.	—sick.
4	—was nigh.	—was at hand.
5	—company	—multitude
9	—two small fishes:	—two fishes:
11	—he distributed to the disciples, and the disciples to them that were set down;	—he distributed to them that were set down;
12	—the fragments that remain,	—the broken pieces that remain over,
14	Then those men, when they had seen the miracle that Jesus did, said, This is of a truth that prophet that should come into the world.	When therefore the people saw the sign which he did, they said, This is of a truth the prophet that cometh into the world.
15	—they would come	—they were about to come

Chap.	Authorized Version.	Revised Version.
17	—went	—were going
18	—arose	—was rising
21	—they went.	—they were going.
22	The day following,	On the morrow
	—whereinto his disciples were entered,	} omitted.
24	—the people	—the multitude
	—they also took shipping,	—they themselves got into the boats,
26	—the miracles,	—signs,
27	Labour	Work
	—endureth	—abideth
28	—What shall we do, that we might work the works of God?	What must we do, that we may work the works of God?
30	—What sign shewest thou then,	—What then doest thou for a sign,
32	—Moses gave you not that bread from heaven;	It was not Moses that gave you the bread out of heaven;
39	And this is the Father's will which hath sent me,	And this is the will of him that sent me,
40	And this is the will of him that sent me,	For this is the will of my Father,
47	—believeth on me	—believeth
49	—and are dead.	—and they died.
51	—which I will give	*omitted.*
53	—ye have no life in you.	—ye have not life in yourselves.
57	—by	—because
58	—your fathers did eat manna, and are dead;	—the fathers did eat, and died:

CHAP.	AUTHORIZED VERSION.	REVISED VERSION.
61	—Doth this offend you?	Doth this cause you to stumble?
69	And we believe and are sure that thou art that Christ, the Son of the living God.	And we have believed and know that thou art the Holy One of God.
70	—Have not I chosen you twelve,	Did not I choose you the twelve,
71	—Judas Iscariot the son of Simon:	—Judas the son of Simon Iscariot,
7 1	—Jewry,	—Judæa,
2	—the Jews' feast of tabernacles	—the feast of the Jews, the feast of tabernacles
4	—shew	—manifest
5	For neither did his brethren believe in him.	For even his brethren did not believe on him.
8	—full come.	—fulfilled.
10	—openly,	—publicly,
12	—people	—multitudes
	—deceiveth the people.	—leadeth the multitude astray.
16	—doctrine	—teaching
17	—will do	—willeth to do
	—of myself.	—from myself.
19	—Why go ye about	—Why seek ye
22	Moses therefore gave unto you circumcision; (not because it is of Moses, but of the fathers;)	For this cause hath Moses given you circumcision (not that it is of Moses, but of the fathers);

Chap.	Authorized Version.	Revised Version.
26	—boldly,	—openly,
31	And many of the people believed on him,	But of the multitude many believed on him;
	—miracles	—signs
35	—will he go unto the dispersed among the Gentiles, and teach the Gentiles?	—will he go unto the Dispersion among the Greeks, and teach the Greeks?
36	—manner of saying	—word
40	Many of the people	Some of the multitude
42	—the town of Bethlehem,	Bethlehem, the village
46	—spake like this man.	—so spake.
47	Then answered them the Pharisees, Are ye also deceived?	The Pharisees therefore answered them, Are ye also led astray?
50	—he that came to Jesus by night,	—he that came to him before,
51	—before it hear him,	—except it first hear from himself
8 6	—have to accuse	—have whereof to accuse
	—as though he heard them not.	} *omitted.*
8	—and wrote	—and with his finger wrote
9	—being convicted by their own conscience,	} *omitted.*
	—standing	—where she was
10	—and saw none but the woman,	} *omitted.*
	—where are those thine accusers?	—where are they?

Chap.	Authorized Version.	Revised Version.
11	—go, and sin no more.	—go thy way; from henceforth sin no more.
13	—record	—witness
14	—Though I bear	Even if I bear
17	—testimony	—witness
19	—ye should	—ye would
20	—laid hands on him;	—took him;
27	—understood	—perceived
31	—my disciples indeed;	—truly my disciples;
34	—servant	—bondservant
37	—hath no place in you.	—hath not free course in you.
38	—which ye have seen with	—which ye heard from
44	—ye will do.	—it is your will to do.
	—abode not	—stood not
54	—honour	—glory
59	—going through the midst of them, and so passed by.	} omitted.
9 6	—the eyes of the blind man	—his eyes
8	—they which before had seen him that he was blind,	—they which saw him aforetime, that he was a beggar,
24	—again	—a second time
	—Give God the praise:	—Give glory to God:
27	—I have told you already,	I told you even now,
30	—a marvellous thing,	—the marvel,
40	And some of the Pharisees	Those of the Pharisees

Chap.		Authorized Version.	Revised Version.
10	1	—sheepfold,	—fold of the sheep,
	4	—his own sheep,	—all his own,
	11	—giveth his life	—layeth down his life
	12	—catcheth them, and scattereth the sheep.	—snatcheth them, and scattereth them :
	13	The hireling fleeth,	—he fleeth
	14	—and am known of mine.	—and mine own know me, even as the Father knoweth me,
	15	As the Father knoweth me,	
	16	—there shall be one fold, and one shepherd.	—they shall become one flock, one shepherd.
	19	—for these sayings.	—because of these words.
	21	—the words of him that hath a devil.	—the sayings of one possessed with a devil.
	24	—make us to doubt?	—hold us in suspense?
	26	—as I said unto you.	*omitted.*
	28	—neither shall any man pluck them out	—and no one shall snatch them out
	29	—to pluck them out of my Father's hand.	—to snatch them out of the Father's hand.
	35	—and the scripture cannot be broken;	—(and the scripture cannot be broken)
	38	—believe,	—understand
	39	—but he escaped	—and he went forth
	40	—where John at first baptized;	—where John was at the first baptizing;
	41	—miracle :	—sign :
11	6	—he abode two days still in the same place	—he abode at that time two days in the place
	8	—the Jews of late sought	—the Jews were but now seeking

Chap.	Authorized Version.	Revised Version.
11	—sleepeth;	—is fallen asleep;
12	—he shall do well.	—he will recover.
19	—to comfort them	—to console them
20	—sat still	—still sat
30	Now Jesus——met him.	(Now Jesus —— met him.)
38	—grave.	—tomb.
41	—from the place where the dead was laid.	} omitted.
42	—the people which stand by	—the multitude which standeth around
45	—had seen the things which Jesus did,	—beheld that which he did,
47	—miracles.	—signs.
50	Nor consider	—nor do ye take account
12 2	—at the table	—at meat
3	—costly,	—precious,
6	—bare	—took away
7	—against the day of my burying hath she kept this.	—Suffer her to keep it against the day of my burying.
9	—Much people of the Jews therefore	The common people therefore of the Jews
12	On the next day much people	On the morrow a great multitude
13	—Blessed is the King of Israel that cometh in the name of the Lord.	Blessed is he that cometh in the name of the Lord, even the King of Israel.
17	—people	—multitude
18	—miracle.	—sign.
24	—corn	—grain

Chap.	Authorized Version.	Revised Version.
25	—shall lose it;	—loseth it;
33	—what death	—by what manner of death
35	—lest darkness come upon you:	—that darkness overtake you not:
37	—miracles	—signs
39	Therefore	For this cause
40	—understand	—perceive
	—and be converted,	And should turn,
42	—among the chief rulers	—even of the rulers
43	—praise	—glory
47	—and believe not,	—and keep them not,
50	—everlasting:	—eternal:
13 2	—supper being ended,	—during supper,
7	—know	—understand
10	—washed	—bathed
17	—happy	—blessed
18	—bread with me	—my bread
19	Now	From henceforth
23	Now there was leaning on Jesus' bosom	There was at the table reclining in Jesus' bosom
24	—that he should ask who it should be of whom he spake.	—and saith unto him, Tell us who it is of whom he speaketh.
25	He then lying on Jesus' breast	He leaning back, as he was, on Jesus' breast
26	Jesus answered, He it is, to whom I shall give a sop, when I have dipped it. And when he had dipped	Jesus therefore answereth, He it is, for whom I shall dip the sop, and give it him. So when he had dip-

Chap.	Authorized Version.	Revised Version.
	the sop, he gave it to Judas Iscariot, the son of Simon.	ped the sop, he taketh and giveth it to Judas, the son of Simon Iscariot.
30	—went immediately out:	—went out straightway:
32	If God be glorified in him,	} *omitted.*
37	—for thy sake.	—for thee.
38	—for my sake?	—for me?
14 4	And whither I go ye know, and the way ye know.	And whither I go, ye know the way.
5	—and how can we know the way?	—how know we the way?
10	—but the Father that dwelleth in me, he doeth the works.	—but the Father abiding in me doeth his works.
14	—I will do it.	—that will I do.
17	—because it seeth him not,	—for it beholdeth him not,
18	—comfortless: I will come to you.	—desolate: I come unto you.
19	—seeth	—beholdeth
22	—how is it	—what is come to pass
25	—being yet present with you.	—while yet abiding with you.
26	—which is	—even
	—Ghost,	—Spirit,
30	Hereafter I will not talk	I will no more speak
15 2	—purgeth	—cleanseth
	—bring forth	—bear

Chap.	Authorized Version.	Revised Version.
3	Now	Already
5	—without me	—apart from me
7	—ye shall ask what ye will,	—ask whatsoever ye will.
9	—continue	—abide
11	—might be full.	—may be fulfilled.
15	Henceforth I call you not servants;	No longer do I call you servants;
16	—ordained	—appointed
	—bring forth	—bear
	—remain:	—abide:
22	—cloke	—excuse
26	—testify	—bear witness
16 1	—be offended.	—be made to stumble.
2	—doeth God service.	—offereth service unto God.
4	—told you,	—spoken unto you,
8	—will reprove the world of sin,	—will convict the world in respect of sin,
11	—is judged.	—hath been judged.
13	—will shew you things to come.	—shall declare unto you the things that are to come.
16	—and ye shall not see me:	—and ye behold me no more;
	—because I go to the Father	} *omitted.*
17	—among themselves,	—one to another,
19	—of that I said,	—concerning this, that I said,
24	—full.	—fulfilled.
25	—time	—hour

Chap.		Authorized Version.	Revised Version.
	27	—came from God.	—came forth from the Father.
	30	—are we sure	—know we
17	2	As thou hast given him power	—even as thou gavest him authority
		—as many as thou hast given him.	—whatsoever thou hast given him.
	3	—and Jesus Christ whom thou hast sent.	—and him whom thou didst send, even Jesus Christ.
	4	—I have finished the work	—having accomplished the work
	8	—have known surely	—knew of a truth
	11	—keep through thine own name	—keep them in thy name
	12	—I have kept, and none of them is lost,	—and I guarded them, and not one of them perished,
	15	—from the evil.	—from the evil one.
	23	—perfect in one;	—perfected into one;
	24	Father, I will that they also, whom thou hast given me, be with me where I am;	Father, that which thou hast given me, I will that, where I am, they also may be with me;
	26	—declared	—made known
		—declare it:	—make it known;
18	1	Cedron,	Kidron,
	3	—band of men	—band of soldiers,
	9	—Of them which thou gavest me have I lost none.	Of those whom thou hast given me I lost not one.
	12	—captain	—chief captain

Chap.		Authorized Version.	Revised Version.
	15	—palace	—court
	19	—doctrine.	—teaching.
	22	—the palm of his hand,	—his hand,
	24	Now Annas had sent him bound	Annas therefore sent him bound
	27	—immediately	—straightway
	28	—hall of judgment:	—palace:
		—judgment hall, (*Also in v.* 33).	—palace,
	30	—malefactor,	—evil-doer,
	38	—I find in him no fault at all.	—I find no crime in him.
19	2	—put on him a purple robe,	—arrayed him in a purple garment;
	3	And said	—and they came unto him, and said,
	4	—fault (*Also in v.* 6).	—crime
	5	—robe.	—garment.
	9	—the judgment hall,	—the palace again,
	12	And from henceforth	Upon this
		—let this man go,	—release this man,
	19	—And the writing was,	And there was written,
	25	—Cleopas,	—Clopas,
	29	—put it	—brought it
	30	—the ghost.	—his spirit.
	31	—besought	—asked
	35	—bare record,	—hath borne witness,
	38	—the body of Jesus.	—away his body.
	40	—clothes	—cloths
	41	-sepulchre,	—tomb

Chap.		Authorized Version.	Revised Version.
	42	—for the sepulchre was nigh at hand.	(for the tomb was nigh at hand)
20	3	—and came to the sepulchre.	—and they went toward the tomb.
	6	—went into the sepulchre,	—entered into the tomb;
	7	—wrapped together	—rolled up
	16	—and saith unto him,	—and saith unto him in Hebrew,
	19	Then the same day at evening,	When therefore it was evening, on that day,
	23	—remit,	—forgive,
		—remitted	—forgiven
	30	—truly	—therefore
21	1	—shewed	—manifested
	3	—caught	—took
	4	—morning was now come,	—day was now breaking,
		—shore:	—beach:
	5	—have ye any meat?	—have ye aught to eat?
	7	—fisher's coat unto him,	—coat about him
	8	—with fishes.	—full of fishes.
	9	As soon then as they were come to land,	So when they got out upon the land,
	11	—yet was not the net broken.	—the net was not rent.
	12	—dine.	—break your fast.
		—ask him,	—inquire of him,
	14	—shewed himself	—was manifested
	15	—dined,	—broken their fast,
		—Jonas, (*Also in vv.* 16 *and* 17).	—John,

Chap.	Authorized Version.	Revised Version.
16	—Feed	—Tend
20	—leaned on	—leaned back on
24	—testifieth	—beareth witness
	—testimony	—witness
25	—Amen.	*omitted.*

THE ACTS.

Chap.	Authorized Version.	Revised Version.
1 1	—of	—concerning
2	—taken	—received
	—commandments unto	—commandment through
3	—many infallible proofs,	—many proofs,
	—being seen of them forty days,	—appearing unto them by the space of forty days,
	—pertaining to	—concerning
4	—commanded	—charged
5	—indeed	—truly
7	—put in his own power.	—set within his own authority.
11	—gazing up	—looking
	—taken	—received
	—as ye have seen him go	—as ye beheld him going
12	—from	—nigh unto
13	—room,	—chamber,
	—Zelotes,	—the Zealot,
	—brother of James.	—son of James.
14	—and supplication	*omitted*.
15	—disciples,	—brethren,
	—(the number of names together were about	(and there was a multitude of persons

Chap.	Authorized Version.	Revised Version.
	an hundred and twenty,)	gathered together, about a hundred and twenty),
16	Men and brethren, this scripture must needs have been fulfilled,	Brethren, it was needful that the scripture should be fulfilled,
17	—with us, and had obtained part of this ministry.	—among us, and received his portion in this ministry.
18	—purchased	—obtained
19	—proper tongue,	—language
		(NOTE:—*vv. 18 and 19 are put in parenthesis*).
20	—bishoprick	—office
23	—appointed	—put forward
	—Barsabas,	—Barsabbas,
25	—by transgression fell,	—fell away,
26	—gave forth their lots;	—gave lots for them;
2 1	—fully come,	—now come,
	—with one accord	—together
3	—cloven tongues	—tongues parting asunder,
6	—when this was noised abroad,	—when this sound was heard,
10	—and strangers of Rome, Jews and proselytes,	—and sojourners from Rome, both Jews and proselytes,
11	Cretes	Cretans
	—wonderful	—mighty
12	—were in doubt,	—were perplexed,
14	—said	—spake forth
	—hearken	—give ear

THE ACTS.

Chap.	Authorized Version.	Revised Version.
17	—come to pass (*Also in v.* 21).	—be
20	—before that great and notable day of the Lord come:	Before the day of the Lord come, That great and notable day:
22	—miracles	—mighty works
23	—ye have taken, and by wicked hands have crucified and slain:	—ye by the hand of lawless men did crucify and slay:
24	—pains	—pangs
25	—foresaw	—beheld
26	—rest in hope:	—dwell in hope:
27	—hell,	—Hades,
	—suffer	—give
28	—joy	—gladness
29	Men and brethren, let me freely speak unto you	Brethren, I may say unto you freely
30	—according to the flesh,	*omitted.*
	—he would raise up Christ to sit on his throne;	—he would set one upon his throne;
31	—seeing this before	—foreseeing this
	—that his soul was not left in hell,	—that neither was he left in Hades,
33	—shed	—poured
35	Until I make thy foes thy footstool.	Till I make thine enemies the footstool of thy feet.
37	—Men and brethren,	—Brethren,
39	—shall call.	—shall call unto him.
40	—untoward	—crooked

Chap.	Authorized Version.	Revised Version.
46	And they, continuing daily	And day by day continuing
	—from house to house, did eat their meat	—at home, they did take their food
47	—And the Lord added to the church daily such as should be saved.	And the Lord added to them day by day those that were being saved.
3 1	—went up	—were going up
2	—gate	—door
3	—asked an alms.	—asked to receive an alms.
6	—rise up and walk.	—walk.
10	And they knew that it was he	—and they took knowledge of him, that it was he.
11	—the lame man which was healed	—he
12	—why marvel ye at this? or why look ye so earnestly on us,	—why marvel ye at this man? or why fasten ye your eyes on us,
13	—Son Jesus;	—Servant Jesus;
	—in the presence	—before the face
	—to let him go.	—to release him.
14	—the Holy one and the Just,	—the Holy and Righteous One,
16	And his name through faith in his name hath made	And by faith in his name hath his name made
18	—that Christ should suffer, he hath so fulfilled.	—that his Christ should suffer, he thus fulfilled.
19	—and be converted,	—and turn again,

Chap.	Authorized Version.	Revised Version.
19	—when the times of refreshing shall come	—that so there may come seasons of refreshing
20	And he shall send Jesus Christ, which before was preached unto you:	—and that he may send the Christ who hath been appointed unto you, even Jesus:
21	—restitution	—restoration
22	For Moses truly said unto the fathers,	Moses indeed said,
23	—shall come to pass,	—shall be,
24	—have likewise foretold	—they also told
25	—children	—sons
	—kindreds	—families
26	—his Son Jesus,	—his Servant,
4 2	—grieved	—sore troubled
	—preached through Jesus	—proclaimed in Jesus
3	—put them in hold unto the next day:	—put them in ward unto the morrow:
4	—was	—came to be
8	—elders of Israel,	—elders,
9	—of the good deed done to the impotent man, by what means he is made whole;	—concerning a good deed done to an impotent man, by what means this man is made whole;
11	This is the stone	He is the stone
16	—done by them	—wrought through them,
22	—was shewed.	—was wrought.
24	Lord, thou art God, which hast made heaven,	O Lord, thou that didst make the heaven
25	Who by the mouth of	—who by the Holy Ghost,

Chap.	Authorized Version.	Revised Version.
	thy servant David hast said, Why did the heathen rage, and the people imagine vain things?	by the mouth of our father David thy servant, didst say, Why did the Gentiles rage, And the peoples imagine vain things?
26	The kings of the earth stood up,	The kings of the earth set themselves in array,
	—Christ.	—Anointed:
27	For of a truth against thy holy child Jesus,	—for of a truth in this city against thy holy Servant Jesus,
28	—determined before to be done.	—foreordained to come to pass.
30	By stretching forth thine hand to heal;	—while thou stretchest forth thy hand to heal;
	—holy child Jesus.	—holy Servant Jesus.
35	—unto every man according as he had need.	—unto each, according as any one had need.
36	—Joses,	—Joseph,
	—consolation,)	—exhortation),
	—of the country of Cyprus,	—a man of Cyprus by race, having a field,
37	Having land,	
5 4	—was it not thine own?	—did it not remain thine own?
6	—wound him up,	—wrapped him round, (Note:—*parenthesis removed from vv.* 12, 13 *and* 14).

Chap.	Authorized Version.	Revised Version.
17	—indignation,	—jealousy,
18	—in the common prison.	—in public ward.
20	—life.	—Life.
21	—early in the morning,	—about daybreak,
	—prison	—prison-house
23	—without before the doors:	—at the doors:
24	—the high priest	*omitted.*
	—they doubted of them	—they were much perplexed concerning them
26	—without violence:	—but without violence;
28	—Did we not straitly command you that ye should not teach in his name?	We straitly charged you not to teach in this name:
29	—ought	—must
31	—forgiveness	—remission
33	—and took counsel	—and were minded
34	—little space;	—little while.
36	—boasting himself	—giving himself out
	—were scattered, and brought to nought.	—were dispersed, and came to nought.
37	—taxing,	—enrolment,
	—much people	—some of the people
	—dispersed.	—scattered abroad.
38	—come to nought:	—be overthrown:
40	—commanded	—charged
41	—shame	—dishonour
42	—in every house,	—at home,
	—preach Jesus Christ.	—preach Jesus as the Christ.

Chap.	Authorized Version.	Revised Version.
6 1	—was multiplied,	—was multiplying,
	—Grecians	—Grecian Jews
2	—It is not reason that we should leave	—It is not fit that we should forsake
3	—honest	—good
	—Holy Ghost	—Spirit
4	—will give ourselves continually to prayer	—will continue stedfastly in prayer
8	—faith	—grace
	—miracles	—signs
10	—resist	—withstand
12	—caught	—seized
13	—blasphemous words	*omitted.*
15	—looking stedfastly on him,	—fastening their eyes on him,
7 2	—Men, brethren, and fathers,	Brethren and fathers
	—Charran,	—Haran,
4	—he removed him	—God removed him
5	—for a possession,	—in possession,
9	—envy,	—jealousy
11	—dearth	—famine
12	—first.	—the first time.
13	—Joseph's kindred was made known	—Joseph's race became manifest
16	—for a sum of money of the sons of Emmor the father of Sychem.	—for a price in silver of the sons of Hamor in Shechem.
17	—had sworn to	—vouchsafed unto
19	—so that they cast out their young children	—that they should cast out their babes
20	In which time	At which season

CHAP.	AUTHORIZED VERSION.	REVISED VERSION.
22	—learned	—instructed
23	—full	—well-nigh
25	—would deliver them:	—was giving them deliverance;
28	—as thou diddest	—as thou killedst
33	—Put off thy shoes	—Loose the shoes
34	—I have seen, I have seen	—I have surely seen
36	He brought them out, after that he had shewed	This man led them forth, having wrought wonders and signs
37	—him shall ye hear.	*omitted.*
39	—would not obey,	—would not be obedient,
41	—offered sacrifice	—brought a sacrifice
44	—fashion	—figure
45	—that came after,	—in their turn,
	—with Jesus into the possession of the Gentiles,	—with Joshua when they entered on the possession of the nations,
46	—desired to find a tabernacle	—asked to find a habitation
48	—temples	—houses
49	—and earth is my footstool:	And the earth the footstool of my feet:
52	—the Just One;	—the Righteous One;
53	—by the disposition of angels,	—as it was ordained by angels,
59	—upon God,	—upon the Lord,
8 1	And at that time there was a great persecution	And there arose on that day a great persecution

Chap.	Authorized Version.	Revised Version.
3	—made havock of the church,	—laid waste the church,
4	—went every where	—went about
5	—and preached Christ unto them.	—and proclaimed unto them the Christ.
6	—hearing and seeing the miracles which he did.	—when they heard, and saw the signs which he did.
9	—bewitched the people	—amazed the people
10	—This man is the great power of God.	—This man is that power of God which is called Great.
11	—they had regard,	—they gave heed
	—bewitched	—amazed
12	—the things concerning	—good tidings concerning
13	—and wondered, beholding the miracles and signs which were done.	—and beholding signs and great miracles wrought, he was amazed.
21	—in the sight of God.	—before God.
22	—pray God,	—pray the Lord,
23	—perceive	—see
25	—preached the word	—spoken the word
26	—which is desert.	—the same is desert.
27	—who had the charge	—who was over
37	And Philip said, If thou believest with all thine heart, thou mayest. And he answered and said, I believe that Jesus Christ is the Son of God.	} *omitted.*

Chap.	Authorized Version.	Revised Version.
39	—and he went	—for he went
40	—preached in all the cities,	—preached the gospel in all the cities,
9 2	—of this way,	—that were of the Way,
3	—as he journeyed, he came near	—as he journeyed, it came to pass that he drew nigh
5	—And the Lord said,	And he said,
	—it is hard for thee to kick against the pricks.	
6	And he trembling and astonished said, Lord, what wilt thou have me to do? And the Lord said unto him,	} *omitted.*
8	—no man:	—nothing;
16	—how great things	—how many things
17	—went his way,	—departed,
21	—destroyed them	—made havock of them
24	—their laying await was known	—their plot became known
25	—let him down by the wall in a basket.	—let him down through the wall, lowering him in a basket.
29	—the Lord Jesus,	—the Lord:
	—the Grecians:	—the Grecian Jews;
31	—rest	—peace,
32	—quarters,	—parts,
33	—and was sick of the palsy.	—for he was palsied.
34	—maketh thee whole:	—healeth thee:

Chap.		Authorized Version.	Revised Version.
	35	—Saron	—Sharon
10	3	—evidently,	—openly,
	4	And when he looked on him, he was afraid,	And he, fastening his eyes upon him, and being affrighted,
	6	—he shall tell thee what thou oughtest to do.	} *omitted.*
	8	And when he had declared all these things	—and having rehearsed all things
	11	—knit at the four corners, and let down to the earth:	—let down by four corners upon the earth:
	12	—and wild beasts,	*omitted.*
	15	—spake	—came
		—that call not thou	—make not thou
	17	—doubted in himself	—was much perplexed in himself
	21	—which were sent unto him from Cornelius;	} *omitted.*
	22	—a just man,	—a righteous man
		—of good report	—well reported of
	25	And as Peter was coming in,	And when it came to pass that Peter entered,
	28	—Ye know	—Ye yourselves know
		—to keep company,	—to join himself
	30	—Four days ago I was fasting until this hour; and at the ninth hour I prayed in my house,	—Four days ago, until this hour, I was keeping the ninth hour of prayer in my house;
		—clothing,	—apparel,

Chap.	Authorized Version.	Revised Version.
32	—who, when he cometh, shall speak unto thee.	} *omitted.*
33	—before God,	—in the sight of God,
35	—is accepted with him.	—is acceptable to him.
36	—preaching peace	—preaching good tidings of peace
37	That word, I say, ye know,	—that saying ye yourselves know,
38	How God anointed Jesus of Nazareth with the Holy Ghost	—even Jesus of Nazareth, how that God anointed him with the Holy Ghost
39	—land	—country
40	—and shewed him openly;	—and gave him to be made manifest,
42	—commanded	—charged
45	—astonished,	—amazed,
48	—the name of the Lord.	—the name of Jesus Christ.
11 4	But Peter rehearsed the matter from the beginning, and expounded it by order unto them,	But Peter began, and expounded the matter unto them in order,
6	—fowls of the air.	—fowls of the heaven.
11	And, behold, immediately there were three men already unto the house where I was, sent from Cæsarea unto me.	And behold, forthwith three men stood before the house in which we were, having been sent from Cæsarea unto me.
12	—nothing doubting.	—making no distinction.

Chap.		Authorized Version.	Revised Version.
	13	—he shewed us	—he told us
	19	—persecution	—tribulation
	20	—Grecians,	—Greeks
	21	—and a great number believed, and turned unto the Lord.	—and a great number that believed turned unto the Lord.
	22	Then tidings of these things	And the report concerning them
	28	—dearth	—famine
		—Claudius Cæsar.	—Claudius.
12	1	—vex	—afflict
	4	—apprehended	—taken
		—Easter	—the Passover
	5	—without ceasing	—earnestly
	6	—would have brought him	—was about to bring him
		—keepers	—guards
	7	—came upon him,	—stood by him,
		—prison :	—cell :
		—and raised him up,	—and awoke him,
	10	—his own accord :	—its own accord :
	13	—to hearken,	—to answer,
	14	—gladness,	—joy,
	15	—constantly affirmed	—confidently affirmed
	16	—opened the door,	—opened,
		—astonished.	—amazed.
	17	—Go shew these things	—Tell these things
	19	—keepers,	—guards,
		—their abode.	—tarried there.
	20	—desired peace ;	—asked for peace,
		—nourished by the king's country.	—fed from the king's country.

Chap.	Authorized Version.	Revised Version.
22	—It is the voice	—The voice
25	—ministry,	—ministration,
13 1	—Simeon	—Symeon
	—Manaen, which had been brought up with Herod	—Manaen the foster-brother of Herod
5	—they had also John to their minister.	—they had also John as their attendant.
7	—the deputy of the country, Sergius Paulus, a prudent man;	—the proconsul, Sergius Paulus, a man of understanding.
8	—deputy (*Also in v.* 12).	—proconsul
9	—set his eyes on him,	—fastened his eyes on him, and said, O full of all guile and all villany, thou son of the devil,
10	And said, O full of all subtility and all mischief, thou child of the devil,	
12	—doctrine	—teaching
13	—loosed from	—set sail from
15	—Ye men and brethren,	—Brethren,
16	—give audience.	—hearken.
17	—dwelt as strangers	—sojourned
19	—he divided their land to them by lot.	—he gave them their land for an inheritance, for about four hundred and fifty years: and after these things he gave them judges until Samuel the prophet.
20	And after that he gave unto them judges about the space of four hundred and fifty years, until Samuel the prophet.	
21	—desired	—asked for
	—by the space	—for the space

Chap.	Authorized Version.	Revised Version.
22	—gave testimony,	—bare witness,
23	—raised	—brought
25	—Whom think ye that I am?	—What suppose ye that I am?
26	Men and brethren,	—Brethren,
	—to you is the word of this salvation sent.	—to us is the word of this salvation sent forth.
29	—sepulchre.	—tomb.
31	—who are	—who are now
32	And we declare unto you glad tidings, how that the promise which was made unto the fathers,	And we bring you good tidings of the promise made unto the fathers, how that God hath fulfilled the same unto our children,
33	God hath fulfilled the same unto us their children,	
34	—the sure mercies of David.	—the holy and sure blessings of David.
35	Wherefore he saith	Because he saith
	—Thou shalt not suffer	—Thou wilt not give
36	For David, after he had served his own generation by the will of God,	For David, after he had in his own generation served the counsel of God,
38	—is preached unto you the forgiveness of sins:	—is proclaimed unto you remission of sins:
41	—though a man declare it	—if one declare it
42	And when the Jews were gone out of the synagogue, the Gentiles besought	And as they went out they besought

Chap.	Authorized Version.	Revised Version.
43	—congregation —religious —persuaded	—synagogue —devout —urged
45	—envy, —and spake against those things which were spoken by Paul, contradicting and blaspheming.	—jealousy, —and contradicted the things which were spoken by Paul, and blasphemed.
46	—waxed bold, —ye put it from you,	—spake out boldly, —ye thrust it from you,
47	—the ends	—the uttermost part
48	—word of the Lord:	—word of God:
49	—published	—spread abroad
50	But the Jews stirred up the devout and honourable women, and the chief men of the city, and raised persecution against Paul and Barnabas, and expelled them out of their coasts.	But the Jews urged on the devout women of honourable estate, and the chief men of the city, and stirred up a persecution against Paul and Barnabas, and cast them out of their borders.
14 2	But the unbelieving Jews stirred up the Gentiles,	But the Jews that were disobedient stirred up the souls of the Gentiles,
3	—abode they —gave testimony	—they tarried there —bare witness
5	—an assault made —to use them despitefully,	—an onset —to entreat them shamefully,

Chap.	Authorized Version.	Revised Version.
6	—were ware	—became aware
9	—stedfastly beholding him,	—fastening his eyes upon him,
	—to be healed,	—to be made whole,
11	—people	—multitudes
12	—Mercurius,	—Mercury,
13	—which was before their city,	—whose temple was before the city,
	—with the people.	—with the multitudes.
14	—clothes,	—garments,
	—the people,	—the multitude,
15	—and preach unto you,	—and bring you good tidings,
	—vanities	—vain things
16	—in times past	—in the generations gone by
17	Nevertheless	And yet
18	—the people,	—the multitudes
19	—who persuaded the people, and having stoned Paul, drew him out of the city,	—and having persuaded the multitudes, they stoned Paul, and dragged him out of the city,
20	—and the next day he departed	—and on the morrow he went forth
21	—and had taught many,	—and had made many disciples,
23	—ordained them	—appointed for them
24	And after they had passed through	And they passed through
25	—preached	—spoken
26	—recommended	—committed
28	And there they abode long time	And they tarried no little time

Chap.	Authorized Version.	Revised Version.
15 1	—manner	—custom
2	—disputation	—questioning
	—they determined	—the brethren appointed
3	—Phenice	—Phœnicia
4	—declared	—rehearsed
5	—command	—charge
7	—disputing,	—questioning,
9	—put no difference between us and them, purifying their hearts	—made no distinction between us and them, cleansing their hearts
11	—even as they.	—in like manner as they.
12	—gave audience to	—hearkened unto
	—declaring what miracles	—rehearsing what signs
13	—Men and brethren,	Brethren,
14	—declared	—rehearsed
16	—fallen down;	—fallen;
17	—saith the Lord, who doeth all these things.	Saith the Lord, who maketh these things known from the beginning of the world.
18	Known unto God are all his works from the beginning of the world.	
19	—sentence	—judgment
21	—of old	—from generations of old
22	Then pleased it the apostles	Then it seemed good to the apostles
	—surnamed Barsabas,	—called Barsabbas,
23	And they wrote letters by them after this manner;	—and they wrote thus by them,

Chap.	Authorized Version.	Revised Version.
23	—elders and brethren	—elder brethren
24	—saying, Ye must be circumcised, and keep the law:	} *omitted.*
	—no such commandment:	—no commandment;
25	—being assembled with one accord,	—having come to one accord,
	—to send chosen men	—to choose out men
27	—by mouth.	—by word of mouth.
29	—offered	—sacrificed
	—ye shall do well.	—it shall be well with you.
33	And after they had tarried there a space, they were let go in peace from the brethren unto the apostles.	And after they had spent some time there, they were dismissed in peace from the brethren unto those that had sent them forth.
34	Notwithstanding it pleased Silas to abide there still.	} *omitted.*
35	—continued	—tarried
36	—Let us go again	—Let us return
	—preached	—proclaimed
	—how they do.	—how they fare.
37	And Barnabas determined to take with them John, whose surname was Mark.	And Barnabas was minded to take with them John also, who was called Mark.
38	—who departed from them	—who withdrew from them

THE ACTS.

Chap.	Authorized Version.	Revised Version.
39	And the contention was so sharp between them,	And there arose a sharp contention,
40	—recommended	—commended
	—the grace of God.	—the grace of the Lord.
16 1	—Timotheus, the son of a certain woman, which was a Jewess, and believed;	—Timothy, the son of a Jewess which believed;
3	—quarters:	—parts:
5	—established	—strengthened
6	—preach	—speak
7	—the Spirit suffered them not.	—the Spirit of Jesus suffered them not.
9	—and prayed him,	—beseeching him,
10	—immediately we endeavoured to go	—straightway we sought to go forth
	—assuredly gathering	—concluding
11	Therefore loosing from Troas,	Setting sail therefore from Troas,
	—we came with	—we made
12	—which is the chief city of that part of Macedonia, and a colony:	—which is a city of Macedonia, the first of the district, a Roman colony:
	—abiding	—tarrying
13	—we went out of the city	—we went forth without the gate
	—where prayer was wont to be made;	—where we supposed there was a place of prayer;
	—which resorted thither.	—which were come together.

Chap.	Authorized Version.	Revised Version.
14	—that she attended	—to give heed
16	—as we went to prayer,	—as we were going to the place of prayer,
17	—which shew unto us	—which proclaim unto you
18	—being grieved,	—being sore troubled,
19	—they caught Paul and Silas, and drew them into the market place	—they laid hold on Paul and Silas, and dragged them into the market place
21	And teach customs,	—and set forth customs
22	—rent off their clothes, and commanded to beat them.	—rent their garments off them, and commanded to beat them with rods.
25	—Paul and Silas prayed, and sang praises unto God: and the prisoners heard them.	—Paul and Silas were praying and singing hymns unto God, and the prisoners were listening to them;
26	—prison	—prison-house
27	And the keeper of the prison awaking out of his sleep,	And the jailor being roused out of sleep,
	—had been fled.	—had escaped.
29	Then he called for a light, and sprang in, and came trembling,	Then he called for lights, and sprang in, and, trembling for fear,
34	—and rejoiced, believing in God with all his house.	—and rejoiced greatly, with all his house, having believed in God.
36	—keeper of the prison	—jailor

Chap.		Authorized Version.	Revised Version.
	36	—depart,	—come forth,
	37	—openly	—publicly,
	39	—desired them to depart	—asked them to go away
17	2	—manner	—custom
	3	—Christ must needs have suffered,	—it behoved the Christ to suffer,
		—whom I preach unto you, is Christ.	—whom, said he, I proclaim unto you, is the Christ.
	4	—believed,	—were persuaded,
	5	—envy,	—jealousy,
		—lewd fellows of the baser sort,	—vile fellows of the rabble,
		—company,	—crowd,
	8	—the people	—the multitude
	9	—and of the other,	—and the rest,
	11	—and searched	—examining
	12	—of honourable women which were Greeks,	—of the Greek women of honourable estate,
	13	—preached	—proclaimed
		—and stirred up the people.	—stirring up and troubling the multitudes.
	14	—as it were to the sea:	—as far as to the sea:
	16	—his spirit was stirred in him, when he saw the city wholly given to idolatry.	—his spirit was provoked within him, as he beheld the city full of idols.
	17	Therefore disputed he in the synagogue	So he reasoned in the synagogue
		—market	—market place
	19	—unto Areopagus,	—unto the Areopagus,
		—doctrine,	—teaching

Chap.	Authorized Version.	Revised Version.
22	—in the midst of Mars' hill,	—in the midst of the Areopagus,
	—too superstitious.	—somewhat superstitious.
23	—beheld your devotions,	—observed the objects of your worship,
	—To the unknown God. Whom therefore ye ignorantly worship, him declare I unto you.	—To an unknown God. What therefore ye worship in ignorance, this set I forth unto you.
25	Neither is worshipped with men's hands,	—neither is he served by men's hands,
26	And hath made of one blood all nations	—and he made of one every nation of men
	—the times before appointed,	—their appointed seasons,
27	—seek the Lord,	—seek God,
29	Forasmuch then as we are	Being then
30	—God winked at;	—God overlooked;
32	—We will hear thee again of this matter.	—We will hear thee concerning this yet again.
33	—departed	—went out
34	Howbeit	But
	—among the which	—among whom
18 1	—Paul departed	—he departed
2	—born in Pontus,	—a man of Pontus by race,
3	—craft,	—trade,
	—occupation	—trade

18. 24   THE ACTS.   127

Chap.	Authorized Version.	Revised Version.
5	—pressed in the spirit,	—constrained by the word,
7	—named Justus,	—named Titus Justus,
8	—the chief ruler	—the ruler
9	Then spake the Lord	And the Lord said
10	—hurt	—harm
11	—continued	—dwelt
12	—the deputy	—proconsul
	—made insurrection with one accord	—with one accord rose up
13	—This fellow	—This man
14	—lewdness,	—villany,
15	—I will be no judge	—I am not minded to be a judge
17	Then all the Greeks took Sosthenes,	And they laid hold on Sosthenes,
18	And Paul after this tarried there yet a good while,	And Paul, having tarried after this yet many days,
19	And he came	And they came
20	—they desired him to tarry longer time with them,	—they asked him to abide a longer time,
21	But bade them farewell,	—but taking his leave of them,
	—I must by all means keep this feast that cometh in Jerusalem:	} *omitted.*
23	—over all the country	—through the region
	—strengthening	—stablishing
24	—born at Alexandria, an eloquent man,	—an Alexandrian by race, a learned man,

Chap.	Authorized Version.	Revised Version.
25	—diligently	—carefully
	—the things of the Lord,	—the things concerning Jesus,
27	—disposed	—minded
	—the brethren wrote, exhorting the disciples to receive him:	—the brethren encouraged him, and wrote to the disciples to receive him:
28	—mightily convinced	—powerfully confuted
19 1	—upper coasts	—upper country
2	—Have ye received the Holy Ghost since ye believed?	—Did ye receive the Holy Ghost when ye believed?
	—whether there be any Holy Ghost.	—whether the Holy Ghost was given.
3	—unto	—into
4	—Christ Jesus.	—Jesus.
8	—disputing	—reasoning
9	—divers were hardened, and believed not,	—some were hardened and disobedient,
	—of that way	—of the Way
	—disputing	—reasoning
10	—by the space	—for the space
	—the Lord Jesus,	—the Lord,
13	—vagabond Jews,	—strolling Jews,
14	—and chief of the priests,	—a chief priest,
16	—overcame them,	—mastered both of them,
18	—confessed, and shewed their deeds.	—confessing and declaring their deeds.
19	Many of them also which used curious arts	And not a few of them which practised curious arts

Chap.	Authorized Version.	Revised Version.
19	—before all men:	—in the sight of all:
23	—about that way.	—concerning the Way.
24	—small gain	—little business
25	—craft	—business
26	Moreover	And
27	So that not only this our craft is in danger to be set at nought;	—and not only is there danger that this our trade come into disrepute;
	—should be despised, and her magnificence should be destroyed,	—be made of no account, and that she should even be deposed from her magnificence,
28	—these sayings,	—this,
30	—would have entered in	—was minded to enter in
31	—certain of the chief of Asia,	—certain also of the chief officers of Asia,
32	—was confused;	—was in confusion;
33	—drew	—brought
34	—knew	—perceived
35	—appeased the people,	—quieted the multitude,
	—is a worshipper of the great goddess Diana,	—is temple-keeper of the great Diana,
36	—spoken against,	—gainsaid,
37	—churches,	—temples
38	—the law is open, and there are deputies: let them implead one another.	—the courts are open, and there are proconsuls: let them accuse one another.
39	But if ye enquire any thing concerning other matters, it	But if ye seek any thing about other matters, it shall be

Chap.	Authorized Version.	Revised Version.
	shall be determined in a lawful assembly.	settled in the regular assembly.
40	For we are in danger to be called in question for this day's uproar, there being no cause whereby we may give an account of this concourse.	For indeed we are in danger to be accused concerning this day's riot, there being no cause for it: and as touching it we shall not be able to give account of this concourse.
20 1	—Paul called unto him the disciples, and embraced them,	—Paul having sent for the disciples and exhorted them, took leave of them,
3	And there abode three months.	And when he had spent three months there,
4	—Sopater of Berea,	—Sopater of Berœa, the son of Pyrrhus;
5	These going before tarried for us at Troas.	But these had gone before, and were waiting for us at Troas.
6	—abode	—tarried
7	—when the disciples came together to break bread, Paul preached unto them, ready to depart on the morrow; and continued his speech until midnight.	—when we were gathered together to break bread, Paul discoursed with them, intending to depart on the morrow; and prolonged his speech until midnight.
8	—where they were	—where we were
9	—being fallen into a deep sleep: and as Paul was long preaching,	—borne down with deep sleep; and as Paul discoursed yet long-

Chap.	Authorized Version.	Revised Version.
	he sunk down with sleep, and fell down from the third loft,	er, being borne down by his sleep he fell down from the third story,
10	—Trouble not yourselves,	—Make ye no ado;
11	When he therefore was come up again, and had broken bread,	And when he was gone up, and had broken the bread,
12	—young man	—lad
13	—to ship,	—to the ship,
	—minding himself to go afoot.	—intending himself to go by land.
16	—by Ephesus, because he would not spend the time in Asia: for he hasted,	—past Ephesus, that he might not have to spend time in Asia; for he was hastening,
18	—Ye know,	—Ye yourselves know,
	—that I came into Asia,	—that I set foot in Asia,
	—at all seasons,	—all the time,
19	—humility	—lowliness
	—and with many tears, and temptations, which befell me by the lying in wait of the Jews:	—and with tears, and with trials which befell me by the plots of the Jews:
20	And how I kept back nothing that was profitable unto you,	—how that I shrank not from declaring unto you anything that was profitable,
	—but have shewed you,	*omitted.*
24	But none of these things move me,	} *omitted.*
	—neither count I my life dear unto myself,	But I hold not my life of any account, as dear unto myself,

Chap.	Authorized Version.	Revised Version.
24	—finish	—accomplish
25	—I have gone	—I went about
26	—I take you to record	—I testify unto you
27	For I have not shunned to declare	For I shrank not from declaring
28	—overseers,	—bishops,
32	And now, brethren,	And now
35	I have shewed you all things,	In all things I gave you an example
38	—they accompanied him	—they brought him on his way
21 1	—after we had gotten from them, and had launched,	—we were parted from them, and had set sail,
2	—finding a ship sailing over	—having found a ship crossing over
	—set forth.	—set sail.
3	—when we had discovered Cyprus,	—when we had come in sight of Cyprus
	—into Syria,	—unto Syria,
4	—who said	—and these said
	—should not go up to	—should not set foot in
5	And when we had accomplished those days,	And when it came to pass that we had accomplished the days,
	—went our way;	—went on our journey;
	—and they all brought us on our way, with wives and children,	—and they all, with wives and children, brought us on our way,
	—shore,	—beach,
6	And when we had taken our leave one	—and bade each other farewell; and we

Chap.	Authorized Version.	Revised Version.
	of another, we took ship;	went on board the ship,
7	—our course	—the voyage
	—we came to	—we arrived at
8	—the next day	—on the morrow
	—that were of Paul's company	} *omitted.*
11	And when he was come unto us,	And coming to us,
13	—What mean ye to weep and to break mine heart?	—What do ye, weeping and breaking my heart?
15	—carriages,	—baggage,
16	—old disciple,	—early disciple,
19	—declared particularly	—rehearsed one by one
22	—the multitude must needs come together:	} *omitted.*
25	—we have written and concluded that they observe no such thing, save only that they keep themselves	—we wrote, giving judgement that they should keep themselves
26	—to signify the accomplishment	—declaring the fulfilment
27	—ended,	—completed,
31	—as they went about	—as they were seeking
	—an uproar.	—confusion.
32	Who immediately took soldiers	And forthwith he took soldiers
33	—demanded	—inquired
34	—cried	—shouted

Chap.	Authorized Version.	Revised Version.
34	—multitude : —tumult,	—crowd : —uproar,
37	—was to be led	—was about to be brought
	—May I speak unto thee? Who said, Canst thou speak Greek?	—May I say something unto thee? And he said, Dost thou know Greek?
38	—madest an uproar, and leddest out into the wilderness four thousand men that were murderers?	—stirred up to sedition and led out into the wilderness the four thousand men of the Assassins?
39	—I am a man which am a Jew of Tarsus, a city in Cilicia,	—I am a Jew, of Tarsus in Cilicia,
	—suffer me	—give me leave
40	—licence,	—leave,
	—tongue,	—language,
22 1	Men, brethren, and fathers,	Brethren and fathers,
2	—they kept the more silence :	—they were the more quiet :
3	I am verily a man which am a Jew, born in Tarsus, a city in Cilicia,	I am a Jew, born in Tarsus of Cilicia,
	—taught	—instructed
	—perfect	—strict
4	—this way	—this Way
5	—went to Damascus,	—journeyed to Damascus,
	—which were there	—which were there

23. 7 THE ACTS. **135**

Chap.	Authorized Version.	Revised Version.
	bound unto Jerusalem,	unto Jerusalem in bonds,
12	—having a good report of all the Jews	—well reported of by all the Jews
14	—chosen	—appointed
	—that Just One,	—the Righteous One,
16	—calling on the name of the Lord.	—calling on his name.
20	—thy martyr Stephen	—Stephen thy witness
	—consenting unto his death, and kept the raiment	—consenting, and keeping the garments
23	—clothes,	—garments,
24	—they cried so	—they so shouted
25	And as they bound him with thongs,	And when they had tied him up with the thongs,
26	—Take heed what thou doest:	—What art thou about to do?
28	—freedom.	—citizenship.
	—I was free born.	—I am a Roman born.
29	—which should have examined him:	—which were about to examine him
30	—he loosed him from his bands,	—he loosed him,
	—to appear,	—to come together,
23 1	—earnestly beholding the council,	—looking stedfastly on the council,
	—Men and brethren,	—Brethren,
3	—after the law,	—according to the law,
6	—the son of a Pharisee:	—a son of Pharisees:
7	—multitude	—assembly

Chap.	Authorized Version.	Revised Version.
9	—cry:	—clamour:
	—but if a spirit or an angel hath spoken to him,	—and what if a spirit hath spoken to him, or an angel?
	—let us not fight against God.	} *omitted.*
11	—Be of good cheer, Paul:	—Be of good cheer:
	—of me	—concerning me
14	—that we will eat nothing until we have slain Paul.	—to taste nothing until we have killed Paul.
15	—as though ye would enquire something more perfectly concerning him:	—as though ye would judge of his case more exactly:
17	—a certain thing	—something
18	—prayed me	—asked me
19	—went with him aside privately, and asked him,	—going aside asked him privately,
20	—somewhat of him more perfectly.	—somewhat more exactly concerning him.
21	—with an oath,	—under a curse,
22	—See thou tell no man that thou hast shewed these things to me.	—Tell no man that thou hast signified these things to me.
23	—to go to Cesarea,	—to go as far as Cæsarea,
24	And provide them beasts, that they may set Paul on,	—and he bade them provide beasts, that they might set Paul thereon,
26	—sendeth greeting.	—greeting.
27	—and should have been	—and was about to be

Chap.	Authorized Version.	Revised Version.
	killed of them : then came I with an army,	slain of them, when I came upon them with the soldiers,
28	—when I would have known the cause	—desiring to know the cause
29	—perceived	—found
30	And when it was told me how that the Jews laid wait for the man, I sent straightway to thee, and gave commandment to his accusers also to say before thee what they had against him. Farewell.	And when it was shewn to me that there would be a plot against the man, I sent him to thee forthwith, charging his accusers also to speak against him before thee.
33	—epistle	—letter
34	And when the governor had read the letter,	And when he had read it,
35	—Herod's judgment hall.	—Herod's palace.
24 1	—Ananias the high priest descended with the elders,	—the high priest Ananias came down with certain elders,
2	—great quietness, and that very worthy deeds are done unto this nation by thy providence,	—much peace, and that by thy providence evils are corrected for this nation,
3	—always,	—in all ways
4	Notwithstanding,	But,
	—I pray thee that thou wouldest hear us	—I intreat thee to hear us
5	—sedition	—insurrections

Chap.	Authorized Version.	Revised Version.
6	Who also hath gone about	—who moreover assayed
	—whom we took,	—on whom also we laid hold :
	—and would have judged according to our law.	
7	But the chief captain Lysias came upon us, and with great violence took him away out of our hands,	*omitted*.
8	Commanding his accusers to come unto thee :	
9	—assented,	—joined in the charge,
10	—answer for myself :	—make my defence :
11	Because that thou mayest understand, that there are yet but twelve days	—seeing that thou canst take knowledge, that it is not more than twelve days
12	—neither raising up the people,	—or stirring up a crowd,
14	—after the way which they call heresy, so worship I the God of my fathers, believing all things which are written in the law and in the prophets :	—after the Way which they call a sect, so serve I the God of our fathers, believing all things which are according to the law, and which are written in the prophets :
15	—they themselves also allow,	—these also themselves look for,
15	—a resurrection of the	—a resurrection both of

Chap.	Authorized Version.	Revised Version.
	dead, both of the just and unjust.	the just and unjust.
18	Whereupon certain Jews from Asia found me	—amidst which they found me
20	—if they have found any evil doing in me,	—what wrong-doing they found,
22	And when Felix heard these things, having more perfect knowledge of that way,	But Felix, having more exact knowledge concerning the Way,
	—I will know the uttermost of your matter.	—I will determine your matter.
23	And he commanded a centurion to keep Paul, and to let him have liberty, and that he should forbid none of his acquaintance to minister or come unto him.	And he gave order to the centurion that he should be kept in charge, and should have indulgence; and not to forbid any of his friends to minister unto him.
24	—in Christ.	—in Christ Jesus.
25	—Felix trembled,	—Felix was terrified,
	—I will call for thee.	—I will call thee unto me.
26	—also	—withal
	—that he might loose him:	} *omitted.*
27	But after two years Porcius Festus came into Felix' room: and Felix, willing to shew the Jews a pleasure, left Paul bound.	But when two years were fulfilled, Felix was succeeded by Porcius Festus; and desiring to gain favour with the Jews, Felix left Paul in bonds.

Chap.	Authorized Version.	Revised Version.
25 1	—ascended from Cæsarea to Jerusalem.	—went up to Jerusalem from Cæsarea.
2	—the high priest and the chief of the Jews	—the chief priests and the principal men of the Jews
4	—should be kept as Cæsarea,	—was kept in charge at Cæsarea,
5	—which among you are able,	—which are of power among you,
	—and accuse this man, if there be any wickedness in him.	—and if there is anything amiss in the man, let them accuse him.
6	—more than ten days,	—not more than eight or ten days,
7	—and laid many and grievous complaints against Paul,	—bringing against him many and grievous charges,
8	While he answered for himself,	—while Paul said in his defence,
	—have I offended any thing at all.	—have I sinned at all.
9	—willing to do the Jews a pleasure,	—desiring to gain favour with the Jews,
11	—an offender,	—a wrong-doer,
	—but if there be none of these things	—but if none of those things is true
14	—left in bonds	—left a prisoner
15	—desiring to have judgment against him.	—asking for sentence against him.
16	—the manner	—the custom
	—to deliver any man to die,	—to give up any man,
	—have licence to answer for himself concern-	—have had opportunity to make his defence

Chap.	Authorized Version.	Revised Version.
	ing the crime laid against him.	concerning the matter laid against him.
17	—come hither,	—come together here,
18	Against whom	Concerning whom,
	—none accusation of such things as I supposed:	—no charge of such evil things as I supposed:
19	—superstition,	—religion,
20	And because I doubted of such manner of questions,	And I, being perplexed how to inquire concerning these things,
21	—to be reserved unto the hearing of Augustus,	—to be kept for the decision of the emperor,
22	—I would also hear the man myself.	—I also could wish to hear the man myself.
24	—have dealt with me,	—made suit to me,
25	—appealed to Augustus,	—appealed to the emperor
27	—the crimes	—the charges
26 1	—and answered for himself:	—and made his defence:
2	—because I shall answer for myself	—that I am to make my defence
5	Which knew me from the beginning,	—having knowledge of me from the first,
7	—instantly	—earnestly
	—hope to come.	—hope to attain.
	—For which hope's sake, king Agrippa, I am accused of the Jews.	And concerning this hope I am accused by the Jews, O king!
8	Why should it be thought a thing incredible	Why is it judged incredible with you,

Chap.	Authorized Version.	Revised Version.
10	—voice	—vote
11	—compelled them to blaspheme;	—I strove to make them blaspheme;
	—strange	—foreign
14	—tongue,	—language,
	—the pricks.	—the goad.
16	—for this purpose	—for to this end
20	But shewed first unto them of Damascus,	—but declared both to them of Damascus first,
	—coasts	—country
	—meet for	—worthy of
21	—caught me	—seized me
	—and went about to kill me.	—and assayed to kill me.
22	—help of God,	—help that is from God,
	—continue	—stand
	—saying none other things than those which the prophets	—saying nothing but what the prophets
23	—he should be the first that should rise from the dead, and should shew light	—he first by the resurrection of the dead should proclaim light
24	—spake for himself,	—made his defence,
	—beside thyself;	—mad;
	—make thee mad.	—turn thee to madness.
25	—noble	—excellent
28	—Almost thou persuadest me to be a Christian.	—With but little persuasion thou wouldest fain make me a Christian.
29	—that not only thou, but	—that whether with lit-

Chap.	Authorized Version.	Revised Version.
	also all that hear me this day, were both almost, and altogether such as I am,	tle or with much, not thou only, but also all that hear me this day, might become such as I am,
30	—when he had thus spoken,	*omitted.*
31	—when they were gone aside, they talked between themselves,	—when they had withdrawn, they spake one to another,
27 1	—unto one named Julius, a centurion of Augustus' band.	—to a centurion named Julius, of the Augustan band.
2	And entering into a ship of Adramyttium, we launched, meaning to sail by the coasts of Asia;	And embarking in a ship of Adramyttium, which was about to sail unto the places on the coast of Asia, we put to sea,
3	—courteously entreated Paul,	—treated Paul kindly,
3	—liberty	—leave
4	And when we had launched	And putting to sea
	—under Cyprus,	—under the lee of Cyprus,
5	—when we had sailed over the sea of Cilicia	—when we had sailed across the sea which is off Cilicia
7	—the wind not suffering us, we sailed under Crete,	—the wind not further suffering us, we sailed under the lee of Crete,
8	And, hardly passing it,	—and with difficulty coasting along it,

Chap.	Authorized Version.	Revised Version.
9	—sailing —the fast	—voyage —the Fast
10	—hurt and much damage,	—injury and much loss,
11	—believed the master	—gave heed to the master
12	—to depart thence	—to put to sea from thence,
	—they might attain to Phenice,	—they could reach Phœnix,
	—and lieth toward the southwest and northwest.	—looking north-east and south-east.
13	—loosing thence, they sailed close by Crete.	—they weighed anchor and sailed along Crete, close in shore.
14	But not long after there arose against it a tempestuous wind called Euroclydon.	But after no long time there beat down from it a tempestuous wind, which is called Euraquilo:
15	—and could not bear up into the wind, we let her drive.	—and could not face the wind, we gave way to it, and were driven.
16	—running under a certain island which is called Clauda, we had much work to come by the boat:	—running under the lee of a small island called Clauda, we were able, with difficulty, to secure the boat:
17	—when they had taken up, they used helps, undergirding the ship; and, fearing lest they should fall into the quicksands, strake sail,	—when they had hoisted it up, they used helps, undergirding the ship; and, fearing lest they should be cast upon the Syrtis, they lowered the gear,

Chap.	Authorized Version.	Revised Version.
18	And we being exceedingly tossed with a tempest, the next day they lightened the ship;	And as we laboured exceedingly with the storm, the next day they began to throw the freight overboard;
20	—in many days appeared,	—shone upon us for many days,
21	And after long abstinence	And when they had been long without food,
	—loosed	—set sail
	—gained this harm	—gotten this injury
22	—but of the ship.	—but only of the ship.
24	—be brought	—stand
	—given	—granted
27	—up and down in Adria,	—to and fro in the sea of Adria,
	—the shipmen deemed	—the sailors surmised
28	—and when they had gone a little further,	—and after a little space,
29	—lest we should have fallen upon rocks,	—lest haply we should be cast ashore on rocky ground,
30	—the shipmen were about to flee	—the sailors were seeking to flee
	—let down the boat	—lowered the boat
33	—that ye have tarried	—that ye wait
34	—I pray you to take some meat:	—I beseech you to take some food:
	—health:	—safety:
36	—and they also took some meat.	—and themselves also took food.
38	—and cast out	—throwing out

Chap.	Authorized Version.	Revised Version.
39	—they discovered a certain creek with a shore, into the which they were minded, if it were possible, to thrust in the ship.	—they perceived a certain bay with a beach, and they took counsel whether they could drive the ship upon it.
40	And when they had taken up the anchors, they committed themselves unto the sea,	And casting off the anchors, they left them in the sea,
	—mainsail	—foresail
	—made toward shore.	—made for the beach.
41	—falling into	—lighting upon
	—the forepart stuck fast,	—the foreship struck
	—the hinder part was broken	—the stern began to break up
43	—willing	—desiring
	—should cast themselves first into the sea, and get to land :	—should cast themselves overboard, and get first to the land :
44	—broken pieces	—other things
28 1	—they	—we
2	—barbarous people	—barbarians
	—little	—common
3	—out of the heat,	—out by reason of the heat,
4	—the venomous beast hang on his hand, they said among themselves,	—the beast hanging from his hand, they said one to another,
	—vengeance	—Justice
5	And	Howbeit
	—felt no harm.	—took no harm.

Chap.	Authorized Version.	Revised Version.
6	—they looked when he should have swollen,	—they expected he would have swollen,
	—but after they had looked a great while, and saw no harm come to him,	—but when they were long in expectation, and beheld nothing amiss come to him,
7	In the same quarters were possessions of the chief man of the island,	Now in the neighbourhood of that place were lands belonging to the chief man of the island,
8	—it came to pass,	—it was so,
	—a bloody flux:	—dysentery:
9	—healed:	—cured:
10	—when we departed, they laded us with such things as were necessary.	—when we sailed, they put on board such things as we needed.
11	—we departed	—we set sail
	—Castor and Pollux.	—The Twin Brothers.
12	—landing	—touching
13	—we fetched a compass, and came to Rhegium:	—we made a circuit, and arrived at Rhegium:
	—blew,	—sprang up,
	—we came the next day	—on the second day we came
14	—desired	—intreated
	—we went toward Rome.	—we came to Rome.
15	—Appii forum, and The three taverns:	—The Market of Appius, and The Three Taverns:
16	—came to	—entered into

Chap.	Authorized Version.	Revised Version.
16	—the centurion delivered the prisoners to the captain of the guard :	*omitted.*
17	—Men and brethren,	—I, brethren,
18	—would have let me go,	—desired to set me at liberty,
20	—have I called for you, to see you, and to speak with you :	—did I intreat you to see and to speak with me :
23	—there came many to him into his lodging ;	—they came to him into his lodging in great number ;
	—expounded and testified the kingdom of God,	—expounded the matter, testifying the kingdom of God,
24	—believed not.	—disbelieved.
27	—should be converted,	—should turn again,
28	—and that they will hear it.	—they will also hear.
29	And when he had said these words, the Jews departed, and had great reasoning among themselves.	*omitted.*
30	—house,	—dwelling,
31	—with all confidence, no man forbidding him.	—with all boldness, none forbidding him.

TO THE ROMANS.

Chap.		Authorized Version.	Revised Version.
1	3	—Jesus Christ our Lord,	*omitted.*
		—made	—born
	4	—the dead :	—the dead ; even Jesus Christ our Lord,
	5	—for obedience to the faith	—unto obedience of faith
		—for his name :	—for his name's sake :
	6	—called of Jesus Christ :	—called to be Jesus Christ's :
	8	—spoken of	—proclaimed
	9	—with my spirit	—in my spirit
		—in my prayers ;	—in my prayers making request,
	10	Making request,	
		—I might have a prosperous journey	—I may be prospered
	12	—that I may be comforted together with you by the mutual faith both of you and me.	—that I with you may be comforted in you, each of us by the other's faith, both yours and mine.
	13	—let	—hindered
	14	—unwise.	—foolish.
	17	—from faith to faith : as it is written, The just shall live by faith.	—by faith unto faith : as it is written, But the righteous shall live by faith.

Chap.	Authorized Version.	Revised Version.
18	—who hold the truth	—who hold down the truth
19	—shewed it	—manifested it
20	—being understood	—being perceived
	—even his eternal power and Godhead; so that they are without excuse:	—even his everlasting power and divinity; that they may be without excuse.
21	—when they knew God,	—knowing God,
	—were thankful;	—gave thanks;
	—imaginations,	—reasonings,
	—foolish	—senseless
24	—gave them up to uncleanness through the lusts of their own hearts, to dishonour their own bodies between themselves:	—gave them up in the lusts of their hearts unto uncleanness, that their bodies should be dishonoured among themselves:
25	Who changed the truth of God into a lie,	—for that they exchanged the truth of God for a lie,
26	—affections:	—passions:
27	—that which is unseemly,	—unseemliness,
	—meet.	—due.
28	—did not like to retain God	—refused to have God
	—convenient;	—fitting;
29	—fornication,	*omitted.*
	—debate,	—strife,
30	—haters of God, despiteful, proud, boasters,	—hateful to God, insolent, haughty, boastful,

Chap.		Authorized Version.	Revised Version.
	31	—implacable,	*omitted.*
	32	—judgment	—ordinance
		—commit	—practise
		—but have pleasure in them that do them.	—but also consent with them that practise them.
2	1	—doest	—dost practise
	2	But we are sure	And we know
		—commit	—practise
	3	—thinkest	—reckonest
		—do such things,	—practise such things,
	6	—deeds:	—works:
	7	—patient continuance	—patience
		—immortality,	—incorruption,
	8	—contentious,	—factious,
		—indignation and wrath,	—shall be wrath and indignation,
	9	—doeth evil	—worketh evil,
		—the Gentile	—the Greek;
		(*Also in v.* 10).	
	12	—sinned in the law	—sinned under law
	15	Which shew	—in that they shew
		—their conscience also bearing witness, and their thoughts the mean while accusing or else excusing one another;	—their conscience bearing witness therewith, and their thoughts one with another accusing or else excusing them;
	17	Behold, thou art called a Jew, and restest in the law, and makest thy boast of God,	But if thou bearest the name of a Jew, and restest upon the law, and gloriest in God,

Chap.		Authorized Version.	Revised Version.
	20	An instructor	—a corrector
	22	—dost thou commit sacrilege?	—dost thou rob temples?
	23	Thou that makest thy boast of the law, through breaking the law	—thou who gloriest in the law, through thy transgression of the law
	25	—verily	—indeed
		—keep	—be a doer of
		—breaker	—transgressor
	26	—righteousness	—ordinances
		—counted	—reckoned
3	2	—chiefly, because that unto them were committed the oracles of God.	—first of all, that they were instructed with the oracles of God.
	3	—did not believe?	—were without faith?
		—unbelief	—want of faith
		—faith of God	—faithfulness of God?
	4	—be true,	—be found true,
		—sayings, and mightest overcome when thou art judged.	—words, And mightest prevail when thou comest into judgment.
	5	—who taketh vengeance? (I speak as a man)	—who visiteth with wrath? (I speak after the manner of men.)
	8	And not rather,	—and why not,
		—damnation	—condemnation
	9	—are we better than they?	—are we in worse case than they?
		—proved both Jews and Gentiles,	—laid to the charge both of Jews and Greeks,

Chap.	Authorized Version.	Revised Version.
12	—gone out of the way,	—turned aside,
	—no, not one.	—no, not so much as one:
19	—may become guilty before God.	—may be brought under the judgement of God:
20	Therefore	—because
21	But now the righteousness of God without the law is manifested,	But now apart from the law a righteousness of God hath been manifested,
22	—difference:	—distinction;
23	—come short	—fall short
25	—through faith in his blood, to declare his righteousness for the remission of sins that are past, through the forbearance of God;	—through faith, by his blood, to shew his righteousness, because of the passing over of the sins done aforetime, in the forbearance of God; for the shewing, I say, of his righteousness at this present season:
26	To declare, I say, at this time his righteousness:	
	—which believeth	—that hath faith
27	Where is boasting then?	Where then is the glorying?
	—By what law?	—By what manner of law?
28	Therefore we conclude that a man is justified by faith without the deeds of the law.	We reckon therefore that a man is justified by faith apart from the works of the law.
30	Seeing it is one God,	—if so be that God is one,

Chap.		Authorized Version.	Revised Version.
3	31	—make void the law	—make the law of none effect
		—yea,	—nay,
4	1	—pertaining	—according
	2	—before God.	—toward God.
	3	—counted	—reckoned
	6	—describeth the blessedness of the man, unto whom God imputeth righteousness without works,	—pronounceth blessing upon the man unto whom God reckoneth righteousness apart from works,
	8	—impute	—reckon
	9	Cometh this blessedness then upon	Is this blessing then pronounced upon
	11	—yet being uncircumcised:	—while he was in uncircumcision:
		—imputed	—reckoned
	12	—being yet uncircumcised:	—in uncircumcision.
	16	Therefore it is of faith, that it might be by grace;	For this cause it is of faith, that it may be according to grace;
	18	Who against hope believed in hope,	Who in hope believed against hope,
	19	And being not weak in faith, he considered not his own body now dead, when he was about an hundred years old, neither yet the deadness of Sarah's womb:	And without being weakened in faith he considered his own body now as good as dead (he being about a hundred years old) and the deadness of Sarah's womb:
	20	He staggered not at	—yea, looking unto the

Chap.	Authorized Version.	Revised Version.
	the promise of God through unbelief;	promise of God, he wavered not through unbelief,
21	—persuaded	—assured
22	And therefore it was imputed to him	Wherefore also it was reckoned unto him
23	—imputed	—reckoned
24	But for us also, to whom it shall be imputed,	—but for our sake also, unto whom it shall be reckoned,
25	—offences	—trespasses
5 .1	—we have peace	—let us have peace
2	—and rejoice in hope	—and let us rejoice in hope
3	—but we glory in tribulations also:	—but let us also rejoice in our tribulations:
4	—experience;	—probation;
5	—maketh not ashamed;	—putteth not to shame
6	—without strength,	—weak,
	—time	—season
7	—yet	—for
9	—from wrath	—from the wrath of God
11	—joy	—rejoice
	—the atonement.	—the reconciliation.
12	Wherefore, as by one	Therefore, as through one
14	—similitude	—likeness
15	—offence,	—trespass,
	—which is by one man,	—of the one man,
16	—offences	—trespasses
17	—by one man's offence	—by the trespass of the one,

Chap.		Authorized Version.	Revised Version.
	18	—by the offence of one	—through one trespass
		—by the righteousness of one	—through one act of righteousness
	20	Moreover the law entered, that the offence might abound.	And the law came in beside, that the trespass might abound;
		—much more abound	—abound more exceedingly:
6	3	Know ye not,	Or are ye ignorant
	5	—we have been planted together in the likeness of his death,	—we have become united with him by the likeness of his death,
	6	—that the body of sin might be destroyed, that henceforth we should not serve sin.	—that the body of sin might be done away, that so we should no longer be in bondage to sin; for he
	7	For he that is dead is freed from sin.	that hath died is justified from sin.
	10	For in that he died,	For the death that he died,
		—but in that he liveth,	—but the life that he liveth,
	11	—through Jesus Christ our Lord.	—in Christ Jesus.
	13	—yield	—present
	16	—yield yourselves servants to obey,	—present yourselves as servants unto obedience,
	17	But God be thanked, that ye were the servants of sin, but ye have obeyed from the heart that form	But thanks be to God, that, whereas ye were servants of sin, ye became obedient from the heart to

Chap.	Authorized Version.	Revised Version.
	of doctrine which was delivered you.	that form of teaching whereunto ye were delivered;
19	—yielded	—presented
	—holiness.	—sanctification.
20	—ye were free from righteousness.	—ye were free in regard of righteousness.
21	—then	—at that time
22	—holiness,	—sanctification
	—eternal	—everlasting
23	—the gift of God	—the free gift of God
7 1	Know ye not,	Or are ye ignorant,
2	—as long as he liveth;	—while he liveth;
	—loosed	—discharged
3	—married (*Also in v.* 4).	—joined
5	—the motions of sins,	—the sinful passions,
	—did work	—wrought
6	—we are delivered	—we have been discharged
	—that being dead wherein we were held;	—having died to that wherein we were holden;
7	—Nay,	—Howbeit,
	—lust,	—coveting,
8	—taking occasion	—finding occasion
	—concupiscence.	—coveting:
	—without the law (*Also in v.* 9).	—apart from the law
10	—was ordained to life,	—was unto life,
11	—deceived me,	—beguiled me,
12	—just,	—righteous,

Chap.	Authorized Version.	Revised Version.
13	—that it might appear	—that it might be shewn to be
15	—I allow not:	—I know not:
	—for what I would, that do I not;	—for not what I would, that do I practise;
18	—but how to perform that which is good I find not.	—but to do that which is good is not.
19	—that I do.	—that I practise.
21	—evil is present with me.	—evil is present.
23	—another	—different
8 1	—who walk not after the flesh, but after the Spirit.	} *omitted*.
3	—and for sin,	—and as an offering for sin,
4	—righteousness	—ordinance
6	For to be carnally minded is death; but to be spiritually minded is life and peace.	For the mind of the flesh is death; but the mind of the spirit is life and peace.
7	—the carnal mind	—the mind of the flesh
15	—Spirit	—spirit
16	—itself	—himself
17	—glorified together.	—glorified with him.
18	—revealed in us.	—revealed to us-ward.
19	—creature (*Also in vv.* 20 *and* 21).	—creation
	—manifestation	—revealing
20	—subjected the same in hope,	—subjected it, in hope that the creation itself
21	Because the creature itself	

Chap.	Authorized Version.	Revised Version.
23	—not only they,	—not only so,
26	Likewise	And in like manner
	—what we should pray for	—how to pray
29	—did predestinate (*Also in v.* 30).	—foreordained
34	—Christ	—Christ Jesus
35	—distress,	—anguish,
38	—things to come,	—things to come, nor powers, nor height,
39	Nor height,	
9 2	—great heaviness and continual sorrow	—great sorrow and unceasing pain
3	—accursed	—anathema.
5	—of whom as concerning the flesh Christ came,	—of whom is Christ as concerning the flesh,
6	—hath taken none effect.	—hath come to nought.
8	—They which are the children of the flesh, these are not the children of God:	—it is not the children of the flesh that are children of God;
9	—At this time	—According to this season
16	—that sheweth mercy.	—that hath mercy.
17	—declared	—published abroad
18	Therefore hath he mercy on whom he will have mercy,	So then he hath mercy on whom he will,
19	—hath resisted	—withstandeth
21	—power	—a right
26	—children	—sons
27	—Though	—If

Chap.	Authorized Version.	Revised Version.
28	For he will finish the work, and cut it short in righteousness: because a short work will the Lord make upon the earth.	—for the Lord will execute his word upon the earth, finishing it and cutting it short.
31	—hath not attained to the law of righteousness.	—did not arrive at that law.
32	—by the works of the law.	—by works.
32	—stumblingstone; (*Also in v.* 33).	—stone of stumbling;
33	—whosoever believeth on him shall not be ashamed.	—he that believeth on him shall not be put to shame.
10 1	—prayer	—supplication
2	—record	—witness
3	—going about	—seeking
5	For Moses describeth the righteousness which is of the law, That the man which doeth those things shall live by them.	For Moses writeth that the man that doeth the righteousness which is of the law shall live thereby.
6	—speaketh on this wise,	—saith thus,
7	—the deep?	—the abyss?
9	That if	—because if
	—the Lord Jesus,	—Jesus as Lord,
11	—be ashamed.	—be put to shame.
12	—difference	—distinction
	—the same Lord over all	—the same Lord is Lord of all,

Chap.		Authorized Version.	Revised Version.
	15	—preach the gospel of peace, and	} omitted.
	16	But they have not all obeyed the gospel.	But they did not all hearken to the glad tidings of good things!
	17	So then faith cometh by hearing, and hearing by the word of God.	So belief cometh of hearing, and hearing by the word of Christ.
	19	—by them that are no people, and by a foolish nation	—with that which is no nation, With a nation void of understanding
11	1	—Hath God cast away his people?	·Did God cast off his people?
	2	—how he maketh intercession to God	—how he pleadeth with God
	4	—reserved to myself	—left for myself
	6	—But if it be of works, then is it no more grace: otherwise work is no more work.	} omitted.
	7	—blinded	—hardened:
	8	—slumber,	—stupor,
	11	—Have they stumbled that they should fall?	—Did they stumble that they might fall?
	12	—the diminishing of them	—their loss
	13	—to you Gentiles,	—to you that are Gentiles.
		—I magnify mine office:	—I glorify my ministry:

Chap.	Authorized Version.	Revised Version.
14	—emulation	—jealousy
16	—the lump is also holy :	—so is the lump :
18	Boast not against the branches. But if thou boast, thou bearest not the root,	—glory not over the branches: but if thou gloriest, it is not thou that bearest the root,
20	—because of unbelief	—by their unbelief
21	—take heed lest he also spare not thee.	—neither will he spare thee.
22	—toward thee, goodness,	—toward thee, God's goodness,
23	—abide	—continue
24	—the olive tree which is wild by nature,	—that which is by nature a wild olive tree,
25	—blindness in part is happened to Israel,	—a hardening in part hath befallen Israel,
28	—concerning	—touching
30	—have not believed God,	—were disobedient to God,
	—through their unbelief:	—by their disobedience,
31	—not believed,	—been disobedient,
	—through your mercy	—by the mercy shewn to you
32	—concluded them all in unbelief,	—shut up all unto disobedience,
33	—finding	—tracing
12 2	—be not conformed to this world :	—be not fashioned according to this world :
3	—but to think soberly,	—but so to think as to think soberly,

Chap.	Authorized Version.	Revised Version.
3	—to every man the measure of faith.	—to each man a measure of faith.
5	—being many,	—who are many,
	—and every one	—and severally
7	—let us wait on our ministering:	—let us give ourselves to our ministry;
8	—simplicity;	—liberality;
9	—dissimulation.	—hypocrisy.
10	Be kindly affectioned one to another with brotherly love;	In love of the brethren be tenderly affectioned one to another;
11	Not slothful in business;	—in diligence not slothful;
12	—instant	—stedfastly
13	Distributing	—communicating
16	Mind not high things,	Set not your mind on high things,
	—to men of low estate.	—to things that are lowly.
17	Recompense	Render
	—Provide things honest	—Take thought for things honourable
18	—live peaceably	—be at peace
19	Dearly beloved, avenge not yourselves, but rather give place unto wrath: for it is written, Vengeance is mine; I will repay, saith the Lord.	Avenge not yourselves, beloved, but give place unto wrath: for it is written, Vengeance belongeth unto me; I will recompense, saith the Lord.
13 2	—resist	—withstand

Chap.	Authorized Version.	Revised Version.
2	—damnation.	—judgment.
3	—Wilt thou then not be afraid of the power?	And wouldest thou have no fear of the power?
4	—a revenger to execute wrath upon him that doeth evil.	—an avenger for wrath to him that doeth evil.
5	—be subject, not only for wrath,	—be in subjection, not only because of the wrath,
6	—God's ministers,	—ministers of God's service,
8	—another:	—his neighbour
9	—Thou shalt not bear false witness,	} *omitted*.
9	—it is briefly comprehended in this saying,	—it is summed up in this word,
10	—fulfilling	—fulfilment
11	And that, knowing the time,	And this, knowing the season,
	—when we believed.	—when we first believed.
13	—rioting	—revelling
	—envying.	—jealousy.
14 1	—but not	—yet not
2	For one believeth that he may eat all things:	One man hath faith to eat all things:
3	—despise	—set at nought
4	—another man's servant?	—the servant of another?
	—master	—lord
	—Yea, he shall be holden up: for God is able to make him stand.	—Yea, he shall be made to stand; for the Lord hath power to make him stand,

Chap.	Authorized Version.	Revised Version.
5	Let every man be fully persuaded	Let each man be fully assured
6	—and he that regardeth not the day, to the Lord he doth not regard it.	} *omitted.*
7	—no man	—none
9	—and rose, and revived,	—and lived again,
12	—every one	—each one
14	—esteemeth	—accounteth
15	But if thy brother be grieved with thy meat, now walkest thou not charitably.	For if because of meat thy brother is grieved, thou walkest no longer in love.
17	—meat and drink;	—eating and drinking,
18	—acceptable	—well-pleasing
20	For meat destroy not the work of God.	Overthrow not for meat's sake the work of God.
	—pure;	—clean;
21	—nor any thing	—nor to do any thing
	—or is offended, or is made weak.	} *omitted.*
22	Hast thou faith?	The faith which thou hast,
	—condemneth	—judgeth
	—alloweth.	—approveth.
23	—damned	—condemned
15 1	We then that are strong	Now we that are strong
2	—every one	—each one
	—for his good to edification.	—for that which is good, unto edifying.

Chap.	Authorized Version.	Revised Version.
3	For even Christ	For Christ also
	—on me.	—upon me.
4	—we	*omitted.*
	—and comfort of the scriptures might have hope.	—and through comfort of the scriptures we might have hope.
5	—and consolation	—and of comfort
	—to be likeminded one toward another,	—to be of the same mind one with another
6	That ye may with one mind and one mouth glorify God, even the Father	—that with one accord ye may with one mouth glorify the God and Father
7	—as Christ also received us,	—even as Christ also received you,
8	Now I say that Jesus Christ was a minister	For I say that Christ hath been made a minister
	—to confirm	—that he might confirm
	—made unto the fathers;	—given unto the fathers,
9	And	—and
	—For this cause I will confess to thee	—Therefore will I give praise unto thee
	—and	—And
11	—and laud him, all ye people.	—And let all the peoples praise him.
12	—Esaias	—Isaiah
	—a root	—the root
	—and he that shall rise to reign .	—And he that ariseth to rule
	—in him	—On him
	—trust.	—hope.
13	—through the power	—in the power

Chap.	Authorized Version.	Revised Version.
14	—ye also	—ye yourselves
15	Nevertheless, brethren, I have written the more boldly unto you in some sort, as putting you in mind,	But I write the more boldly unto you in some measure, as putting you again in remembrance,
	—is given to me	—was given me
16	That	—that
	—the minister of Jesus Christ to the Gentiles,	—a minister of Christ Jesus unto the Gentiles,
	—be acceptable,	—be made acceptable
17	I have therefore whereof I may glory through Jesus Christ in those things which pertain to God.	I have therefore my glorying in Christ Jesus in things pertaining to God.
18	—of those things which Christ hath not wrought by me, to make the Gentiles obedient,	—of any things save those which wrought through me, for the obedience of the Gentiles,
19	Through mighty signs and wonders, by the power of the Spirit of God;	—by word and deed, in the power of signs and wonders, in the power of the Holy Ghost;
	—unto	—even unto
	—Christ.	—Christ;
20	Yea, so have I strived	—yea, making it my aim so
	—was named,	—was already named,
	—lest I should build	—that I might not build
21	But, as it is written,	—but, as it is written,

Chap.	Authorized Version.	Revised Version.
21	—To whom he was not spoken of, they shall see; —and they that have	—They shall see, to whom no tidings of him came, —And they who have
22	For which cause also I have been much hindered	Wherefore also I was hindered these many times
23	But now having no more place in these parts, and having a great desire these many years to come unto you;	—but now, having no more any place in these regions, and having these many years a longing to come unto you,
24	Whensoever I take my journey into Spain, I will come to you: for I trust to see you in my journey, and to be brought on my way thitherward by you, if first I be somewhat filled with your company.	whensoever I go unto Spain (for I hope to see you in my journey, and to be brought on my way thitherward by you, if first in some measure I shall have been satisfied with your company)
25	But now I go unto Jerusalem to minister	—but now, I say, I go unto Jerusalem, ministering
26	For it hath pleased them —the poor saints which	For it hath been the good pleasure —the poor among the saints that
27	It hath pleased them verily; —their duty is also	Yea, it hath been their good pleasure; —they owe it to them also
28	—performed —I will come by you into Spain.	—accomplished —I will go on by you unto Spain.

Chap.	Authorized Version.	Revised Version.
29	—I am sure that, —of the gospel	—I know that, *omitted.*
30	—for the Lord Jesus Christ's sake, —for the love	—by our Lord Jesus Christ, —by the love
31	That I may —that do not believe —service —accepted of	—that I may —that are disobedient —ministration —acceptable to
32	That I may come unto you with joy by the will of God, and may with you be refreshed.	—that I may come unto you in joy through the will of God, and together with you find rest.
16 2	—as becometh saints, —business —and of myself also.	—worthily of the saints, —matter —and of mine own self.
3	—Priscilla —helpers	—Prisca —fellow-workers
5	Likewise greet —Achaia	—and salute —Asia
6	Greet —on us.	Salute —on you.
9	—helper	—fellow-worker
17	—offences —and avoid them.	—occasions of stumbling, —and turn away from them.
18	—Lord Jesus Christ, —by good words and fair speeches deceive the hearts of the simple.	—Lord Christ, —by their smooth and fair speech beguile the hearts of the innocent.

Chap.	Authorized Version.	Revised Version.
19	—on your behalf :	—over you :
	—simple concerning evil.	—simple unto that which is evil.
20	—Amen.	*omitted.*
23	—chamberlain	—treasurer
24	The grace of our Lord Jesus Christ be with you all. Amen.	*omitted.*
25	—which was kept secret since the world began,	—which hath been kept in silence through times eternal,
	—everlasting	—eternal
27	To God only wise, be glory through Jesus Christ for ever. Amen.	—to the only wise God, through Jesus Christ, to whom be the glory for ever. Amen.
	¶ Written to the Romans from Corinthus, and sent by Phebe servant of the church at Cenchrea.	*omitted.*

I. CORINTHIANS.

CHAP.	AUTHORIZED VERSION.	REVISED VERSION.
1 4	—on your behalf, —by Jesus Christ;	—concerning you, —in Christ Jesus;
8	—that ye may be blameless	—that ye may be unreproveable
10	—perfectly joined together	—perfected together
11	—declared unto me of you,	—signified unto me concerning you,
12	—I say,	—I mean,
13	—in the name	—into the name
15	—I had baptized in mine own name.	—ye were baptized into my name.
17	—of none effect.	—void.
18	—preaching —are saved	—word —are being saved
19	—and will bring to nothing the understanding of the prudent.	And the prudence of the prudent will I reject.
21	For after that in the wisdom of God the world by wisdom knew not God, it pleased God	For seeing that in the wisdom of God the world through its wisdom knew not God, it was God's good pleasure
22	For the Jews require a sign,	Seeing that Jews ask for signs,
26	—ye see	—behold

Chap.	Authorized Version.	Revised Version.
27	—to confound the wise;	—that he might put to shame them that are wise;
	—to confound the things that are mighty;	—that he might put to shame the things that are strong;
29	—in his presence.	—before God.
2 1	—declaring unto you the testimony	—proclaiming to you the mystery
4	—with enticing words of man's wisdom,	—in persuasive words of wisdom,
6	—nor of the princes of this world, that come to nought:	—nor of the rulers of this world, which are coming to nought:
7	—even the hidden wisdom, which God ordained before the world unto our glory:	—even the wisdom that hath been hidden, which God foreordained before the worlds unto our glory:
8	—princes	—rulers
9	—Eye hath not seen, nor ear heard, neither have entered into the heart of man, the things which God hath prepared for them that love him.	Things which eye saw not, and ear heard not, And which entered not into the heart of man, Whatsoever things God prepared for them that love him.
11	—knoweth no man,	—none knoweth,
13	—Holy Ghost	—the Spirit
14	—discerned.	—judged.
16	—may	—should

Chap.		Authorized Version.	Revised Version.
3	2	—for hitherto	—for
	3	—envying,	—jealousy
		—and divisions,	*omitted.*
		—walk as men?	—walk after the manner of men?
	4	—are ye not carnal?	—are ye not men?
	5	Who then is Paul, and who is Apollos, but ministers by whom ye believed, even as the Lord gave to every man?	What then is Apollos? and what is Paul? Ministers through whom ye believed; and each as the Lord gave to him.
	8	—every man	—each
	9	—labourers together with God:	—God's fellow-workers:
	10	—every man	—each man
	12	—on this foundation	—on the foundation
		—precious stones,	—costly stones,
	13	—the fire shall try every man's work	—the fire itself shall prove each man's work
	17	—defile	—destroyeth
	18	—seemeth to be wise	—thinketh that he is wise
	21	—no man	—no one
4	4	—by myself;	—against myself;
	5	—every man have praise	—each man have his praise
	6	—that ye might learn in us not to think of men above that which is written,	—that in us ye might learn not to go beyond the things which are written;
	7	—from another?	*omitted.*
	8	Now ye are full, now	Already ye are filled,

Chap.	Authorized Version.	Revised Version.
	ye are rich, ye have reigned as kings without us: and I would to God ye did reign,	already ye are become rich, ye have reigned without us: yea and I would that ye did reign,
9	—as it were appointed to death:	—as men doomed to death:
10	—ye are honourable, but we are despised.	—ye have glory, but we have dishonour.
12	And labour,	—and we toil,
	—we suffer it:	—we endure;
13	—unto this day.	—even until now.
14	—but as my beloved sons I warn you.	—but to admonish you as my beloved children.
15	—instructors	—tutors
16	—followers	—imitators
17	—who is my beloved son, and faithful in the Lord,	—who is my beloved and faithful child in the Lord,
18	—I would not come	—I were not coming
19	—speech	—word
5 1	—reported commonly	—actually reported
	—so much as named among	—even among
3	—have judged already, as though I were present, concerning him that hath so done this deed,	—have already, as though I were present, judged him that hath so wrought this thing,
7	—For even Christ our passover is sacrificed for us:	For our passover also hath been sacrificed, even Christ:

Chap.	Authorized Version.	Revised Version.
11	—railer,	—reviler,
13	—Therefore put away from among yourselves that wicked person.	Put away the wicked man from among yourselves.
6 1	—another,	—his neighbour,
	—unjust,	—unrighteous,
4	—judgments of	—to judge
	—set them	—do ye set them
	—least esteemed	—of no account
5	I speak to your shame.	I say this to move you to shame.
	—that there is not a wise man among you?	—that there cannot be found among you one wise man,
	—judge	—decide
7	Now therefore there is utterly a fault among you, because ye go to law one with another.	Nay, already it is altogether a defect in you, that ye have lawsuits one with another.
	—why do ye not rather suffer yourselves to be defrauded?	—why not rather be defrauded?
8	—ye do wrong,	—but ye yourselves do wrong,
9	—mankind,	—men,
13	—destroy	—bring to nought
14	—by his own power.	—through his power.
16	What? know ye not	Or know ye not
	—two,	—The twain,
20	—and in your spirit, which are God's.	} *omitted*.

Chap.	Authorized Version.	Revised Version.
7 1	—ye wrote unto me:	—ye wrote:
2	Nevertheless, to avoid fornication,	But, because of fornications,
3	—due benevolence:	—her due:
5	—to fasting	*omitted.*
6	But I speak this by permission,	But this I say by way of permission,
7	But every man hath his proper gift of God,	Howbeit each man hath his own gift from God,
9	—if they cannot contain,	—if they have not continency,
10	—I command,	—I give charge,
11	—and let not the husband put away his wife.	—and that the husband leave not his wife.
12	—a wife that believeth not,	—an unbelieving wife,
	—be pleased (*Also in v.* 13).	—is content
	—put her away.	—leave her.
13	—an husband that believeth not,	—an unbelieving husband,
	—leave him.	—leave her husband.
14	—by the husband:	—in the brother:
16	—O man,	—O husband,
17	—every	—each
21	Art thou called being a servant?	Wast thou called being a bondservant?
	—mayest be made free,	—canst become free,
22	—servant,	—bondservant,
	—freeman:	—freedman:
26	—this is good for the	—this is good by reason

Chap.	Authorized Version.	Revised Version.
	present distress, I say, that it is good for a man so to be.	of the present distress, namely, that it is good for a man to be as he is.
28	—Nevertheless such shall have trouble in the flesh: but I spare you.	—Yet such shall have tribulation in the flesh: and I would spare you.
29	—the time is short: it remaineth, that both	—the time is shortened, that henceforth both
32	—without carefulness. —careth (*Also in v.* 33).	—to be free from cares. —is careful
34	—The unmarried woman careth	—She that is unmarried is careful
35	—comely,	—seemly,
36	—uncomely towards his virgin,	—unseemly towards his virgin daughter,
37	—over —and hath so decreed in his heart that he will keep his virgin, doeth well.	—as touching —and hath determined this in his own heart, to keep his own virgin daughter, shall do well.
38	—he that giveth her in marriage doeth well;	—both he that giveth his own virgin daughter in marriage doeth well;
39	The wife is bound by the law as long	A wife is bound for so long
40	—if she so abide,	—if she abide as she is,
8 1	Now as touching things offered unto idols,	Now concerning things sacrificed to idols:

Chap.	Authorized Version.	Revised Version.
1	—charity edifieth.	—love edifieth.
4	—an idol is nothing	—no idol is anything
6	—we in him;	—we unto him;
	—we by him.	—we through him.
7	—for some with conscience of the idol unto this hour	—but some, being used until now to the idol,
10	—of him which is weak	—if he is weak,
	—which are offered	—sacrificed
11	—shall the weak brother perish, for whom Christ died?	—he that is weak perisheth, the brother for whose sake Christ died.
12	But when ye sin so against the brethren, and wound their weak conscience,	And thus, sinning against the brethren, and wounding their conscience when it is weak,
13	—to offend, I will eat no flesh while the world standeth, lest I make my brother to offend.	—to stumble, I will eat no flesh for evermore, that I make not my brother to stumble.
9. 2	—doubtless	—at least
3	Mine answer	My defence
4	Have we not power	Have we no right
5	—a sister	*omitted.*
	—a wife, as well as other apostles,	—a wife that is a believer, even as the rest of the apostles,
7	Who goeth a warfare any time	What soldier ever serveth

Chap.	Authorized Version.	Revised Version.
8	Say I not these things as a man?	Do I speak these things after the manner of men?
9	—muzzle the mouth of the ox that treadeth	—muzzle the ox when he treadeth
	—Doth God take care for oxen?	Is it for the oxen that God careth,
10	—For our sakes, no doubt, this is written:	—Yea, for our sake it was written:
	—and that he that thresheth in hope should be partaker of his hope.	—and he that thresheth, to thresh in hope of partaking.
11	—thing	—matter
12	If others be partakers of this power over you, are not we rather? Nevertheless we have not used this power; but suffer all things, lest we should hinder the gospel of Christ.	If others partake of this right over you, do not we yet more? Nevertheless we did not use this right; but we bear all things, that we may cause no hindrance to the gospel of Christ.
13	—holy	—sacred
	—live	—eat
	—are partakers with the altar?	—have their portion with the altar?
14	—preach	—proclaim
15	—neither have I written these things, that it should be so done unto me:	—and I write not these things that it may be so done in my case:
17	—willingly,	—of mine own will,

Chap.	Authorized Version.	Revised Version.
17	—a dispensation of the gospel is committed unto me.	—I have a stewardship intrusted to me.
18	—Verily that, —that I abuse not my power in the Gospel.	—That, —so as not to use to the full my right in the gospel.
19	—yet have I made myself servant unto all,	—I brought myself under bondage to all,
20	—as under the law, that I might gain	—as under the law, not being myself under the law, that I might gain
23	And this I do —partaker thereof with you.	And I do these things —a joint partaker thereof.
24	—So run	—Even so run
25	—striveth for the mastery —obtain	—striveth in the games —receive
27	—I keep under my body, and bring it into subjection: —a castaway.	—I buffet my body, and bring it into bondage: —rejected.
10 4	—Rock	—rock
5	But with many of them	Howbeit with most of them
9	—Christ, —were destroyed of (*Also in v.* 10).	—the Lord, —perished by
11	—for ensamples: —the world	—by way of example; —the ages
13	—but such as is common to man:	—but such as man can bear:

Chap.	Authorized Version.	Revised Version.
13	—bear it.	—endure it.
16	—the communion	—a communion
17	For we being many are one bread, and one body:	—seeing that we, who are many, are one bread, one body:
18	—are not they	—have not they
	—partakers	—communion
20	—fellowship	—communion
23	—for me,	*omitted.*
24	—but every man another's wealth.	—but each his neighbour's good.
28	—This is offered in sacrifice unto idols,	—This hath been offered in sacrifice,
	—for the earth is the Lord's, and the fulness thereof:	*omitted.*
29	—judged of another man's conscience?	—judged by another conscience?
32	—none offence,	—no occasion of stumbling,
	—Gentiles,	—Greeks,
11 1	—followers	—imitators
2	—brethren,	*omitted.*
	—keep the ordinances,	—hold fast the traditions,
5	—uncovered	—unveiled
	—for that is even all one	—for it is one and the same thing
6	—covered,	—veiled,
7	—to cover his head,	—to have his head veiled,
10	—to have power	—to have a sign of authority

Chap.	Authorized Version.	Revised Version.
11	Nevertheless	Howbeit
13	—uncovered ?	—unveiled ?
14	—shame	—dishonour
17	Now in this that I declare unto you	But in giving you this charge,
20	When ye come together therefore into one place, this is not to eat the Lord's supper.	When therefore ye assemble yourselves together, it is not possible to eat the Lord's supper:
22	—and shame them	—and put them to shame
24	—which is broken for you :	—which is for you :
25	After the same manner also he took the cup, when he had supped,	In like manner also the cup, after supper,
26	—ye do shew	—ye proclaim
28	—examine	—prove
29	—drinketh damnation to himself, not discerning the Lord's body.	—judgment unto himself, if he discern not the body.
30	—and many sleep.	—and not a few sleep.
31	—would judge ourselves,	—discerned ourselves,
33	—tarry	—wait
34	—that ye come not together unto condemnation.	—that your coming together be not unto judgement.
	—when	—whensoever
12 2	—ye were Gentiles,	—when ye were Gentiles
	—even as they were led.	—howsoever ye might be led.
3	—no man speaking by the Spirit of God	—no man speaking in the Spirit of God

Chap.	Authorized Version.	Revised Version.
	calleth Jesus accursed:	saith, Jesus is anathema;
3	—Holy Ghost.	—Holy Spirit.
6	—operations,	—workings,
	—all in all.	—all things in all.
8	—by the same Spirit;	—according to the same Spirit:
13	—Gentiles,	—Greeks,
18	—every one	—each one
23	—members	—parts
27	—and members in particular.	—and severally members thereof.
28	—diversities	—divers kinds.
31	But covet earnestly the best gifts: and yet shew I unto you a more excellent way.	But desire earnestly the greater gifts. And a still more excellent way shew I unto you.
13 1	Though (*Also in vv.* 2 *and* 3).	If
	—charity, (*And in subsequent verses*).	—love,
	—tinkling	—clanging
2	—understand	—know
5	—seeketh not her own, is not easily provoked, thinketh no evil;	—seeketh not its own, is not provoked, taketh not account of evil;
6	—iniquity,	—unrighteousness,
	—in the truth;	—with the truth;
8	—fail;	—be done away;
	—vanish away.	—be done away.

Chap.	Authorized Version.	Revised Version.
11	—understood	—felt
12	—glass,	—mirror,
	—I am known.	—I have been known.
14 1	—charity,	—love;
	—desire	—desire earnestly
2	—in an unknown tongue (*Also in subsequent verses*).	—in a tongue
	—understandeth him;	—understandeth;
3	—to edification, and exhortation, and comfort.	—edification, and comfort, and consolation.
6	—by revelation, or by knowledge, or by prophesying, or by doctrine?	—by way of revelation, or of knowledge, or of prophesying, or of teaching?
7	—sound,	—a voice,
8	—to the battle?	—for war?
10	—and none of them	—and no kind
11	Therefore if I know not	If then I know not
12	—forasmuch as ye are zealous	—since ye are zealous
	—excel	—abound
16	—occupieth the room	—filleth the place
	—understandeth	—knoweth
19	—by my voice	*omitted.*
20	—understanding:	—mind:
21	—With men of other tongues and other lips	—By men of strange tongues and by the lips of strangers
	—and yet for all that they will not hear me,	—and not even thus will they hear me,

Chap.	Authorized Version.	Revised Version.
22	—to them that believe not :	—to the unbelieving :
	—but prophesying serveth not for them that believe not, but for them which believe.	—but prophesying is for a sign, not to the unbelieving, but to them that believe.
23	—come together into one place,	—assembled together,
	—those that are unlearned, or unbelievers,	—men unlearned or unbelieving,
24	—one that believeth not, or one unlearned, he is convinced of all,	—one unbelieving or one unlearned, he is reproved by all,
25	—and report that God is in you of a truth.	—declaring that God is among you indeed.
26	—doctrine,	—teaching,
27	—by course;	—in turn;
29	—two or three, and let the other judge.	—by two or three, and let the others discern.
30	If any thing be revealed to another that sitteth by, let the first hold his peace.	But if a revelation be made to another sitting by, let the first keep silence.
33	—the author of confusion,	—a God of confusion,
34	—but they are commanded to be under obedience,	—but let them be in subjection,
35	—a shame	—shameful
39	—covet	—desire earnestly
15 1	Moreover, brethren, I declare unto you	Now I make known unto you, brethren,

Chap.	Authorized Version.	Revised Version.
2	—if ye keep in memory what I preached unto you,	—I make known, I say, in what words I preached it unto you, if ye hold it fast,
4	—that he rose again the third day	—that he hath been raised on the third day
5	—was seen of	—appeared to
6	—unto this present,	—until now,
7	After that, he was seen of James;	—then he appeared to James;
10	—was not in vain;	—was not found vain;
15	—we have testified	—we witnessed
	—that the dead rise not.	—that the dead are not raised.
19	—hope	—hoped
	—miserable.	—pitiable.
20	—and become	*omitted.*
	—that slept.	—that are asleep.
23	—every man	—each
24	—put down	—abolished
26	—destroyed	—abolished
27	—put all things under his feet.	—put all things in subjection under his feet.
	—put under him, it is manifest	—in subjection, it is evident
	—which did put all things under him.	—who did subject all things unto him.
28	—shall be subdued	—have been subjected
31	—by your rejoicing	—by that glorying in you, brethren,
32	—what advantageth it	—what doth it profit me?

Chap.	Authorized Version.	Revised Version.
	me, if the dead rise not? let us eat and drink;	If the dead are not raised, let us eat and drink,
33	—evil communications	—Evil company
34	—to your shame.	—to move you to shame.
35	—some man	—some one
	—what body	—what manner of body
36	—fool,	—foolish one,
37	—other grain:	—other kind;
38	—to every seed his own body.	—to each seed a body of its own.
39	—kind of flesh of men,	—flesh of men,
44	—There is a natural body, and there is a spiritual body.	—If there is a natural body, there is also a spiritual body.
45	—was made a quickening spirit.	—became a life-giving spirit.
46	—and afterward that	—then that
47	—the Lord from heaven.	—of heaven.
51	—shew	—tell
54	—be brought	—come
55	O death, where is thy sting? O grave, where is thy victory?	O death, where is thy victory? O death, where is thy sting?
56	—strength	—power
16 2	—as God hath prospered him, that there be no gatherings when I come.	—as he may prosper, that no collections be made when I come.
3	—come,	—arrive,
	—to bring your liberality	—to carry your bounty
4	—that I go also,	—for me to go also,

Chap.	Authorized Version.	Revised Version.
6	—and winter with you,	—or even winter,
	—bring me	—set me forward
7	For I will not see you	For I do not wish to see you
11	—conduct him forth	—set him forward on his journey
	—I look for him	—I expect him
12	—I greatly desired him	—I besought him much
	—but his will was not at all to come at this time; but he will come when he shall have convenient time.	—and it was not at all his will to come now; but he will come when he shall have opportunity.
14	Let all your things be done in charity.	Let all that ye do be done in love.
15	—addicted themselves to the ministry of the saints,)	—set themselves to minister unto the saints),
16	That ye submit yourselves unto such, and to every one that helpeth with us, and laboureth.	—that ye also be in subjection unto such, and to every one that helpeth in the work and laboureth.
17	I am glad of	I rejoice at
19	—Priscilla	—Prisca
22	—the Lord Jesus Christ,	—the Lord,
	¶ The first epistle to the Corinthians was written from Philippi by Stephanas, and Fortunatus, and Achaicus, and Timotheus.	} omitted.

II. CORINTHIANS.

Chap.	Authorized Version.	Revised Version.
1 1	—all Achaia:	—the whole of Achaia:
4	—tribulation,	—affliction,
	—trouble,	—affliction,
5	—in us, so our consolation also aboundeth by Christ.	—unto us, even so our comfort also aboundeth through Christ.
6	—consolation and salvation, which is effectual in the enduring of the same sufferings which we also suffer: or whether we be comforted, it is for your consolation and salvation.	—comfort and salvation; or whether we be comforted, it is for your comfort, which worketh in the patient enduring of the same sufferings which we also suffer:
7	—so shall ye be also of the consolation.	—so also are ye of the comfort.
8	—of our trouble which came to us in Asia, that we were pressed out of measure, above strength,	—concerning our affliction which befell us in Asia, that we were weighed down exceedingly, beyond our power,
9	But we had the sentence of death in ourselves,	—yea, we ourselves have had the answer of death within ourselves,
10	—in whom we trust that	—on whom we have set

Chap.	Authorized Version.	Revised Version.
	he will yet deliver us;	our hope that he will also still deliver us;
11	—by prayer for us,	—on our behalf by your supplication;
12	—rejoicing	—glorying
	—in simplicity and godly sincerity,	—in holiness and sincerity of God,
	—we have had our conversation in the world,	—we behaved ourselves in the world,
13	—or acknowledge;	—or even acknowledge;
	—I trust	—I hope
14	—rejoicing,	—glorying,
16	—to be brought on my way	—to be set forward on my journey
17	—did I use lightness?	—did I shew fickleness?
18	—true,	—faithful,
20	For all the promises of God in him are yea, and in him Amen,	For how many soever be the promises of God, in him is the yea: wherefore also through him is the Amen,
23	Moreover I call God for a record	But I call God for a witness
	—I came not as yet	—I forbare to come
24	—dominion	—lordship
2 1	—in heaviness.	—with sorrow.
3	—this same unto you,	—this very thing,
4	—be grieved,	—be made sorry,
5	—grief, he hath not grieved me,	—sorrow, he hath caused sorrow not to me,
	—that I may not overcharge you all.	—(that I press not too heavily) to you all.

Chap.	Authorized Version.	Revised Version.
11	Lest Satan should get an advantage of us:	—that no advantage may be gained over us by Satan:
12	—to preach Christ's gospel,	—for the gospel of Christ,
13	—rest in my spirit,	—relief for my spirit,
14	—causeth us to triumph in Christ,	—leadeth us in triumph in Christ,
15	—that perish:	—that are perishing:
3 1	—or letters of commendation from you?	—or from you?
3	Forasmuch are ye are manifestly declared to be the epistle of Christ	—being made manifest that ye are an epistle of Christ,
	—but in fleshy tables of the heart.	—but in tables that are hearts of flesh.
4	—trust	—confidence
5	—to think	—to account
6	—able ministers of the new testament;	—sufficient as ministers of a new covenant;
7	—was glorious,	—came with glory,
	—his countenance;	—his face;
	—was to be done away:	—was passing away:
10	—had no glory	—hath not been made glorious
	—excelleth.	—surpasseth.
11	—is done away was glorious,	—passeth away was with glory,
	—is glorious.	—is in glory.
12	Seeing then that we have such hope,	Having therefore such a hope,

Chap.		Authorized Version.	Revised Version.
	12	—plainness	—boldness
	13	—to the end of that which is abolished:	—on the end of that which was passing away:
	14	—blinded:	—hardened:
		—untaken away	—unlifted;
	17	—that Spirit:	—the Spirit:
	18	—with open face beholding as in a glass the glory of the Lord, are changed into the same image from glory to glory, even as by the Spirit of the Lord.	—with unveiled face reflecting as a mirror the glory of the Lord, are transferred into the same image from glory to glory, even as from the Lord the Spirit.
4	2	—dishonesty,	—shame,
	3	—be hid, it is hid to them that are lost:	—is veiled, it is veiled in them that are perishing:
	4	—them which believe not,	—the unbelieving,
		—glorious gospel of Christ,	—gospel of the glory of Christ,
		—should shine unto them.	—should not dawn upon them.
	5	—the Lord;	—as Lord,
	6	—For God, who commanded the light to shine out of darkness, hath shined	Seeing it is God, that said, Light shall shine out of darkness, who shined
	7	—excellency	—exceeding greatness
		—of us.	—from ourselves;
	8	We are troubled on	—we are pressed on

Chap.	Authorized Version.	Revised Version.
	every side, yet not distressed;	every side, yet not straitened;
9	Persecuted,	—pursued,
	—cast down,	—smitten down,
10	—of the Lord Jesus,	—of Jesus,
15	—that the abundant grace might through the thanksgiving of many redound to the glory of God.	—that the grace, being multiplied through the many, may cause the thanksgiving to abound unto the glory of God.
16	For which cause	Wherefore
	—perish,	—is decaying,
17	—a far more exceeding and eternal weight of glory;	—more and more exceedingly an eternal weight of glory;
5 2	—earnestly desiring	—longing
	—house	—habitation
4	—mortality	—what is mortal
5	—selfsame	—very
6	—confident, (*Also in v.* 8).	—of good courage,
8	—present	—at home
9	Wherefore we labour, that, whether present or absent, we may be accepted of him.	Wherefore also we make it our aim, whether at home or absent, to be well-pleasing unto him.
10	—appear	—be made manifest
	—in his body,	—in the body,
11	—terror	—fear
	—trust	—hope

Chap.	Authorized Version.	Revised Version.
12	—but give you occasion to glory	—but speak as giving you occasion of glorying
	—somewhat	—wherewith
13	—we be sober, it is for your cause.	—we are of sober mind, it is unto you.
14	—that if one died for all, then were all dead:	—that one died for all, therefore all died;
19	—not imputing their trespasses unto them;	—not reckoning unto them their trespasses,
20	—as though God did beseech you by us: we pray you in Christ's stead,	—as though God were intreating by us: we beseech you on behalf of Christ,
6 1	We then, as workers together with him, beseech you also	And working together with him we intreat also
2	—I have heard thee in a time accepted,	At an acceptable time I hearkened unto thee,
	—accepted time;	—acceptable time;
3	—offence	—occasion of stumbling
	—ministry	—ministration
4	—But in all things approving ourselves	—but in every thing commending ourselves,
5	—in (*And in three subsequent verses*).	—by
8	—honour	—glory
12	—bowels.	—affections.
13	—in the same,	—in like kind
14	—righteousness with unrighteousness?	—righteousness and iniquity?

Chap.		Authorized Version.	Revised Version.
	15	—what part hath he that believeth with an infidel?	—what portion hath a believer with an unbeliever?
7	1	—filthiness	—defilement
	2	Receive us;	Open your hearts to us:
		—we have defrauded no man.	—we took advantage of no man.
	3	I speak not this	I say it not
		—to die and live with you.	—to die together and live together.
	4	—of you:	—toward you,
		—I am exceeding joyful in all our tribulation.	—I overflow with joy in all our affliction.
	5	—rest,	—relief,
		—troubled	—afflicted
	6	—God, that comforteth those that are cast down,	—he that comforteth the lowly, even God,
	7	—consolation	—comfort
		—earnest desire,	—longing,
		—your fervent mind toward me;	—your zeal for me;
	8	—with a letter, I do not repent, though I did repent:	—with my epistle, I do not regret it, though I did regret;
		—perceive	—see
		—though it were but	—though but
	9	—manner, that ye might receive damage	—sort, that ye might suffer loss
	10	—not to be repented of:	—a repentance which bringeth no regret:

Chap.	Authorized Version.	Revised Version.
11	—carefulness	—earnest care
	—vehement desire,	—longing,
	—revenge!	—avenging!
	—clear	—pure
12	—but that our care for you in the sight of God might appear unto you.	—but that your earnest care for us might be made manifest unto you in the sight of God.
13	Therefore we were comforted in your comfort: yea, and exceedingly the more joyed we	Therefore we have been comforted: and in our comfort we joyed the more exceedingly
14	—boasted	—gloried
	—I am not ashamed;	—I was not put to shame;
	—boasting,	—glorying
15	—abundant	—abundantly
16	I rejoice therefore that I have confidence in you in all things.	I rejoice that in every thing I am of good courage concerning you.
8 1	—we do you to wit	—we make known to you
2	—a great trial of affliction	—much proof of affliction
3	For to their power, I bear record,	For according to their power, I bear witness,
	—they were willing of themselves;	—they gave of their own accord,
4	Praying us with much intreaty that we would receive the	—beseeching us with much intreaty in regard of this grace

Chap.	Authorized Version.	Revised Version.
	gift, and take upon us the fellowship of the ministering	and the fellowship in the ministering
5	And this they did,	—and this,
6	—desired	—exhorted
	—begun,	—made a beginning before,
	—finish	—complete
7	—diligence,	—earnestness,
8	—but by occasion of the forwardness of others, and to prove	—but as proving through the earnestness of others
10	—advice :	—judgment :
	—who had begun before, not only to do, but also to be forward a year ago.	—who were the first to make a beginning a year ago, not only to do, but also to will.
11	Now therefore perform the doing of it;	But now complete the doing also;
	—a performance also out of that which ye have.	—the completion also out of your ability.
12	For if there be first a willing mind,	For if the readiness is there,
	—accepted	—acceptable
13	For I mean not that other men be eased, and ye burdened :	For I say not this, that others may be eased, and ye distressed :
17	—but being more forward,	—but being himself very earnest,
18	—whose praise is in the gospel	—whose praise in the gospel is spread
19	—chosen	—appointed

Chap.	Authorized Version.	Revised Version.
19	—with this grace,	—in the matter of this grace,
	—and declaration of your ready mind:	—and to shew our readiness:
20	—in this abundance	—in the matter of this bounty
21	Providing for honest things,	—for we take thought for things honourable,
22	—diligent	—earnest
	—upon the great confidence which I have	—by reason of the great confidence which he hath in you.
23	—fellowhelper concerning you:	—fellow-worker to you-ward;
	—or our brethren be enquired of,	—or our brethren,
24	Wherefore shew ye to them, and before the churches,	Shew ye therefore unto them in the face of the churches
	—boasting	—glorying
9 2	—the forwardness of your mind, for which I boast of you	—your readiness, of which I glory on your behalf
	—Achaia was ready a year ago; and your zeal hath provoked very many.	—Achaia hath been prepared for a year past; and your zeal hath stirred up very many of them.
3	—boasting	—glorying
	—in this behalf;	—in this respect;
	—ready:	—prepared:
4	Lest haply	—lest by any means,

Chap.	Authorized Version.	Revised Version.
4	—should be ashamed in this same confident boasting.	—should be put to shame in this confidence.
5	—exhort	—intreat
	—your bounty whereof ye had notice before,	—your aforepromised bounty,
	—covetousness.	—extortion.
7	Every man according as he purposeth in his heart, so let him give;	Let each man do according as he hath purposed in his heart;
9	—dispersed	—scattered
	—remaineth	—abideth
10	—ministereth	—supplieth
	—both minister bread for your food,	—and bread for food,
	—your seed sown,	—your seed for sowing,
11	—bountifulness, which causeth	—liberality, which worketh
12	—supplieth the wants of the saints,	—filleth up the measure of the wants of the saints,
13	Whiles by the experiment of this ministration they glorify God for your professed subjection unto the gospel of Christ, and for your liberal distribution unto them, and unto all men;	—seeing that through the proving of you by this ministration they glorify God for the obedience of your confession unto the gospel of Christ, and for the liberality of your contribution unto

Chap.	Authorized Version.	Revised Version.
14	And by their prayer for you,	them and unto all; while they themselves also, with supplication on your behalf,
10 1	—beseech	—intreat
	—who in presence am base among you,	—I who in your presence am lowly among you,
	—bold	—of good courage
2	—that I may not be bold when I am present with that confidence, wherewith I think to be bold	—that I may not when present shew courage with the confidence wherewith I count to be bold
3	—after the flesh:	—according to the flesh
4	—carnal,	—of the flesh,
	—pulling	—casting
6	—revenge	—avenge
7	—Do ye look on things after the outward appearance?	—Ye look at the things that are before your face.
	—let him of himself think this again,	—let him consider this again with himself,
8	—boast	—glory
	—which the Lord hath given us for edification, and not for your destruction,	—(which the Lord gave for building you up, and not for casting you down),
10	—powerful;	—strong;
	—contemptible.	—of no account.
11	—think	—reckon
12	For we dare not make ourselves of the number, or compare ourselves	For we are not bold to number or compare ourselves

Chap.	Authorized Version.	Revised Version.
	—are not wise.	—are without understanding.
13	—boast of things	—glory
	—of the rule which God hath distributed to us, a measure to reach even unto you.	—of the province which God apportioned to us as a measure, to reach even unto you.
14	—beyond our measure,	—overmuch,
	—in preaching the gospel of Christ:	—in the gospel of Christ:
15	Not boasting of things	—not glorying
	—when your faith is increased, that we shall be enlarged by you according to our rule abundantly,	—as your faith groweth, we shall be magnified in you according to our province unto further abundance,
16	—in the regions beyond you, and not to boast in another man's line of things made ready to our hand.	—unto the parts beyond you, and not to glory in another man's province in regard of things ready to our hand.
11 1	Would to God ye could bear with me a little in my folly: and indeed bear with me.	Would that ye could bear with me in a little foolishness: and indeed bear with me.
2	—chaste	—pure
3	—through his subtilty,	—in his craftiness,
	—from the simplicity that is in Christ.	—from the simplicity and the purity that is toward Christ.
4	—another	—a different
	—ye might well bear	—ye do well to bear
5	—suppose	—reckon

Chap.	Authorized Version.	Revised Version.
6	—but we have been thoroughly made manifest among you in all things.	—nay, in every thing we have made it manifest among all men to you-ward.
7	Have I committed an offence	Or did I commit a sin
	—freely?	—for nought?
8	—to do you service.	—that I might minister unto you;
9	—and wanted, I was chargeable to no man: for that which was lacking to me the brethren which came from Macedonia supplied:	—and was in want, I was not a burden on any man; for the brethren, when they came from Macedonia, supplied the measure of my want;
10	—boasting	—glorying
13	—such	—such men
	—transforming	—fashioning
14	—is transformed	—fashioneth himself
15	—be transformed	—fashion themselves
16	—a fool;	—foolish;
	—if otherwise,	—but if ye do,
	—boast	—glory
17	—foolishly,	—in foolishness,
	—boasting.	—glorying.
19	For ye suffer fools gladly, seeing ye yourselves are wise.	For ye bear with the foolish gladly, being wise yourselves.
20	—suffer, if a man bring you into bondage,	—bear with a man, if he bringeth you into bondage,
	—if a man take of you,	—if he taketh you captive,

Chap.	Authorized Version.	Revised Version.
21	I speak as concerning reproach,	I speak by way of disparagement,
23	—(I speak as a fool)	—(I speak as one beside himself)
	—in prisons more frequent,	—in prisons more abundantly,
26	—waters,	—rivers,
	—by the heathen,	—from the Gentiles,
27	In weariness and painfulness,	—in labour and travail,
28	—that which cometh upon me daily, the care of all the churches.	—there is that which presseth upon me daily, anxiety for all the churches.
29	—who is offended,	—who is made to stumble,
30	—infirmities.	—weakness.
32	—kept the city of the Damascenes with a garrison, desirous to apprehend me:	—guarded the city of the Damascenes, in order to take me:
12 1	It is not expedient for me doubtless to glory.	I must needs glory, though it is not expedient;
2	—above fourteen	—fourteen
3	—or out of the body, I cannot tell:	—or apart from the body, I know not;
4	—paradise,	—Paradise,
5	Of such an one will I glory: yet of myself I will not glory, but in mine infirmities.	On behalf of such a one will I glory: but on mine own behalf I will not glory, save in my weaknesses.

Chap.	Authorized Version.	Revised Version.
6	—a fool;	—foolish;
	—think	—account
7	And lest I should be exalted above measure through the abundance of the revelations,	And by reason of the exceeding greatness of the revelations—wherefore, that I should not be exalted overmuch,
	—above measure.	—overmuch.
8	For	Concerning
9	—strength	—power
	—infirmities,	—weaknesses,
	—power	—strength
10	Therefore I take pleasure in infirmities, in reproaches,	Wherefore I take pleasure in weaknesses, in injuries,
11	—a fool in glorying;	—foolish:
12	—deeds.	—works.
13	—to other churches,	—to the rest of the churches,
	—burdensome (*Also in v.* 14).	—a burden
15	—spent for you; though the more abundantly I love you, the less I be loved.	—spent for your souls. If I love you more abundantly, am I loved the less?
17	—make a gain	—take advantage
18	—desired	—exhorted
19	Again, think ye that we excuse ourselves unto you?	Ye think all this time that we are excusing ourselves unto you.
20	—lest,	—lest by any means,
	—lest there be debates,	—lest by any means

Chap.	Authorized Version.	Revised Version.
	envyings, wraths, strifes,	there should be strife, jealousy, wraths, factions,
21	—that I shall bewail many which have sinned already,	—and I should mourn for many of them that have sinned heretofore,
13 1	—two or three witnesses	—two witnesses or three
2	I told you before, and foretell you, as if I were present	I have said beforehand, and I do say beforehand, as when I was present
	—to all other,	—to all the rest,
3	—mighty	—powerful
5	Examine yourselves,	Try your own selves,
	—except ye be reprobates?	—unless indeed ye be reprobate.
7	—honest,	—honourable,
9	—we are glad,	—we rejoice,
	—and this also we wish, even your perfection.	—this we also pray for, even your perfecting.
10	Therefore	For this cause
	—that I may not when present deal sharply,	—lest being present I should use sharpness,
	—power	—authority
	—to edification, and not to destruction.	—for building up, and not for casting down.
11	—Be perfect, be of good comfort,	—Be perfected; be comforted;

Chap.	Authorized Version.	Revised Version.
12	Greet	Salute
14	—Amen.	*omitted.*
	¶ The second epistle to the Corinthians was written from Philippi, a city of Macedonia, by Titus and Lucas.	*omitted.*

TO THE GALATIANS.

	The Epistle of Paul the Apostle to the Galatians.	The Epistle of Paul to the Galatians.
Chap.	Authorized Version.	Revised Version.
1 1	—(not of men, neither by man, but by Jesus Christ,	—(not from men, neither through man, but through Jesus Christ,
4	—God and our Father:	—our God and Father:
6	—soon	—quickly
	—another gospel:	—a different gospel;
7	—another;	—another gospel:
8	—accursed. (*Also in v. 9*).	—anathema.
10	—I yet pleased men,	—I were still pleasing men,
11	But I certify you, brethren, that the gospel	For I make known to you, brethren, as touching the gospel
12	—but by the revelation	—but it came to me through revelation
13	—my conversation	—my manner of life
	—wasted it:	—made havock of it:
14	And profited in the Jews' religion above many my equals in mine own nation,	—and I advanced in the Jews' religion beyond many of mine own age among my countrymen,
15	—it pleased God,	—it was the good pleasure of God,

Chap.	Authorized Version.	Revised Version.
16	—heathen;	—Gentiles;
18	—to see Peter, and abode with him	—to visit Cephas, and tarried with him
20	Now the things	Now touching the things
21	Afterwards	Then
22	And was unknown	And I was still unknown
23	—which once he destroyed.	—of which he once made havock;
2 1	—fourteen years after	—after the space of fourteen years
2	—communicated unto them	—laid before them
	—reputation,	—repute,
4	—unawares brought in,	—privily brought in,
5	—by subjection,	—in the way of subjection,
6	But of these who seemed to be somewhat,	But from those who were reputed to be somewhat
	—for they who seemed to be somewhat in conference added nothing to me:	—they, I say, who were of repute imparted nothing to me:
8	—wrought effectually in Peter	—wrought for Peter
	—the same was mighty in me toward the Gentiles:)	—wrought for me also unto the Gentiles);
9	—who seemed	—who were reputed
	—the heathen,	—the Gentiles,

Chap.	Authorized Version.	Revised Version.
10	—the same which I also was forward to do.	—which very thing I was also zealous to do.
11	—Peter	—Cephas
	—I withstood him to the face, because he was to be blamed.	—I resisted him to the face, because he stood condemned.
13	—the other Jews	—the rest of the Jews
14	—Peter	—Cephas
18	—I make myself	—I prove myself
20	I am	I have been
21	—frustrate	—make void
	—is dead in vain.	—died for nought.
3 1	—that ye should not obey the truth,	} *omitted.*
	—hath been evidently set forth, crucified among you?	—was openly set forth crucified?
3	—made perfect by the flesh?	—perfected in the flesh?
4	—if it be yet in vain.	—if it be indeed in vain.
5	—ministereth	—supplieth
6	—accounted	—reckoned
7	—children	—sons
8	—heathen	—Gentiles
11	—The Just	—The Righteous
12	—The man that doeth	—He that doeth
13	—being made	—having become
15	—if it be confirmed, no man disannulleth,	—when it hath been confirmed, no man maketh it void,
16	—made.	—spoken,

14

Chap.	Authorized Version.	Revised Version.
17	—before of God in Christ, —which was —that it should make	—beforehand by God, —which came —so as to make
18	—gave it	—hath granted it
19	Wherefore then serveth the law?	What then is the law?
21	—have given life,	—make alive,
22	But the scripture hath concluded all under sin,	Howbeit the scripture hath shut up all under sin,
23	—kept	—kept in ward
24	—schoolmaster (*Also in v.* 25).	—tutor
25	—after	—now
26	—children	—sons
28	There is —ye are all one	There can be —ye are all one man
4 1	—servant,	—bondservant,
2	—tutors and governors	—guardians and stewards
3	Even so we —elements	So we also, —rudiments
4	—made	—born
7	—no more a servant, —an heir of God through Christ.	—no longer a bondservant, —an heir through God.
8	Howbeit then, when ye knew not God, ye did service	Howbeit at that time, not knowing God, ye were in bondage
9	—after that ye have known God,	—that ye have come to know God,

Chap.	Authorized Version.	Revised Version.
9	—elements,	—rudiments,
	—desire again to be in bondage?	—desire to be in bondage over again?
10	—times,	—seasons,
11	—lest	—lest by any means
12	—ye have not injured me at all.	—Ye did me no wrong:
13	—through infirmity	—because of an infirmity
	—at the first.	—the first time:
14	And my temptation which was in my flesh	—and that which was a temptation to you in my flesh
15	—the blessedness ye spake of?	—that gratulation of yourselves?
	—record, that, if it had been possible,	—witness, that, if possible,
16	Am I therefore become	So then am I become
17	They zealously affect you, but not well; yea, they would exclude you, that ye might affect them.	They zealously seek you in no good way; nay, they desire to shut you out, that ye may seek them.
18	—zealously affected always in a good thing,	—zealously sought in a good matter at all times,
19	—I travail in birth again	—I am again in travail
20	I desire	I could wish
	—I stand in doubt of you.	—I am perplexed about you.
22	—bondmaid,	—handmaid,
23	But he who was of the bondwoman	Howbeit the son by the handmaid
	—was born	—is born

Chap.	Authorized Version.	Revised Version.
23	—but he of the freewoman was by promise.	—but the son by the freewoman is born through promise.
24	—these are	—these women are
	—which gendereth to bondage,	—bearing children unto bondage,
25	—and is	—for she is
26	—which is the mother of us all.	—which is our mother.
27	—for the desolate hath many more children than she which hath an husband.	For more are the children of the desolate than of her which hath the husband.
30	Nevertheless	Howbeit
	—bondwoman	—handmaid
	—shall not be heir	—shall not inherit
31	So then,	Wherefore,
	—the free.	—the freewoman.
5 1	Stand fast therefore in the liberty wherewith Christ hath made us free,	With freedom did Christ set us free: stand fast therefore,
3	—that is circumcised,	—that receiveth circumcision,
4	Christ is become of no effect unto you, whosoever of you are justified by the law; ye are fallen from grace.	Ye are severed from Christ, ye who would be justified by the law; ye are fallen away from grace.
5	—by faith.	*omitted.*
6	—faith which worketh by love.	—faith working through love.

Chap.	Authorized Version.	Revised Version.
7	—did run	—were running
10	—in you	—to you-ward
11	—why do I yet suffer persecution? then is the offence of the cross ceased.	—why am I still persecuted? then hath the stumblingblock of the cross been done away. I would that they which unsettle you would even cut themselves off.
12	I would they were even cut off which trouble you.	
13	—liberty;	—freedom;
	—but by love serve one another.	—but through love be servants one to another.
16	This I say then,	But I say,
17	—ye cannot	—ye may not
19	—which are these; Adultery, fornication, uncleanness, lasciviousness,	—which are these, fornication, uncleanness, lasciviousness, idolatry, sorcery, enmities, strife, jealousies, wraths, factions, divisions, heresies, envyings, drunkenness, revellings,
20	Idolatry, witchcraft, hatred, variance, emulations, wrath, strife, seditions, heresies,	
21	Envyings, murders, drunkenness, revellings,	
	—I tell you before, as I have also told you in time past,	—I forewarn you, even as I did forewarn you,
	—do	—practise
22	—gentleness,	—kindness,
	— faith,	—faithfulness,
24	—are Christ's	—are of Christ Jesus

Chap.	Authorized Version.	Revised Version.
24	—the affections and lusts.	—the passions and the lusts thereof.
25	—let us also walk in the Spirit.	—by the Spirit let us also walk.
26	—desirous of vain glory,	vainglorious,
6 1	—a fault,	—any trespass,
	—considering thyself	—looking to thyself,
4	—have rejoicing in himself alone, and not in another.	—have his glorying in regard of himself alone, and not of his neighbour.
5	—every man	—each man
8	—life everlasting	—eternal life.
10	As we have therefore opportunity, let us do good unto all men,	So then, as we have opportunity, let us work that which is good toward all men,
11	Ye see how large a letter	See with how large letters
12	—constrain	—compel
	—only lest they should suffer persecution	—only that they may not be persecuted
14	But God forbid that I should glory,	But far be it from me to glory,
15	For in Christ Jesus neither circumcision availeth any thing,	For neither is circumcision any thing,
16	—according to this rule,	—by this rule,
17	—for I bear in my body the marks of the Lord Jesus.	—for I bear branded on my body the marks of Jesus.
	¶ Unto the Galatians written from Rome.	} *omitted.*

TO THE EPHESIANS.

Chap.	Authorized Version.	Revised Version.
1 4	According as he hath chosen us	—even as he chose us
	—blame	—blemish
5	—predestinated	—foreordained
	—of children	—as sons
6	—wherein he hath made us accepted in the beloved.	—which he freely bestowed on us in the Beloved:
7	—sins,	—our trespasses,
8	Wherein he hath abounded	—which he made to abound
9	—which he hath purposed in himself:	—which he purposed in him unto a dispensation
10	That in the dispensation	
	—he might gather together in one all things in Christ,	—to sum up all things in Christ,
	—even in him:	—in him, I say, in whom also we were made a heritage, having been foreordained
11	In whom also we have obtained an inheritance, being predestinated	
12	That we	—to the end that we
	—who first trusted in Christ.	—we who had before hoped in Christ:

Chap.	Authorized Version.	Revised Version.
13	In whom ye also trusted, after that ye heard	—in whom ye also, having heard
	—in whom also after that ye believed,	—in whom, having also believed
14	—the purchased possession,	—God's own possession,
15	Wherefore	For this cause
	—and love unto all the saints,	—which is among you, and which ye shew toward all the saints,
18	The eyes of your understanding being enlightened;	—having the eyes of your heart enlightened,
19	—his mighty power,	—the strength of his might
20	—set him	—made him to sit
21	—principality, and power, and might,	—rule, and authority, and power,
22	—put all things	—put all things in subjection
2 1	And you hath he quickened, who were dead in trespasses and sins;	And you did he quicken, when ye were dead through your trespasses and sins,
2	—in time past	—aforetime
	—children	—sons
3	Among whom also we all had our conversation in times past	—among whom we also all once lived
5	—in sins,	—through our trespasses,
	—ye are	—have ye been
6	—together,	—with him,

Chap.	Authorized Version.	Revised Version.
9	—lest any man should boast.	—that no man should glory.
10	—unto good works, which God hath before ordained	—for good works, which God afore prepared
11	—that ye being in time past	—that aforetime ye, the Gentiles in the flesh,
12	That at that time ye were without Christ, being aliens	—that ye were at that time separate from Christ, alienated
13	—ye who sometimes	—ye that once
14	—between us;	*omitted.*
17	—and to them	—and peace to them
19	—foreigners,	—sojourners,
20	—Jesus Christ	—Christ Jesus
21	—all the building	—each several building,
3 1	—Jesus Christ for you Gentiles,	—Christ Jesus in behalf of you Gentiles,—
4	—ye may understand my knowledge	—ye can perceive my understanding
5	—ages	—generations
6	That the Gentiles should be fellow-heirs, and of the same body, and partakers	—to wit, that the Gentiles are fellow-heirs, and fellow-members of the body, and fellow-partakers
7	—by the effectual working	—according to the working
9	—fellowship	—dispensation
	—from the beginning of the world	—from all ages
	—by Jesus Christ:	*omitted.*
10	—by the church	—through the church

Chap.	Authorized Version.	Revised Version.
12	—with confidence by the faith of him.	—in confidence through our faith in him.
13	—I desire	—I ask
	—which is	—which are
14	—of our Lord Jesus Christ,	} *omitted.*
15	Of whom the whole family	—from whom every family
16	—to be strengthened with might	—that ye may be strengthened with power
	—inner man;	—inward man;
17	—that ye,	—to the end that ye,
18	—able	—strong
	—depth and height;	—height and depth,
21	—by Christ Jesus throughout all ages, world without end. Amen.	—and in Christ Jesus unto all generations for ever and ever. Amen.
4 1	—worthy of the vocation	—worthily of the calling
3	Endeavouring	—giving diligence
6	—above all,	—over all,
	—in you all.	—in all.
7	—unto every one of us is given grace	—unto each one of us was the grace given
9	(Now that he ascended,	(Now this, He ascended,
11	—gave some, apostles;	—gave some to be apostles;
12	—for the work of the ministry, for the edifying	—unto the work of ministering, unto the building up

Chap.	Authorized Version.	Revised Version.
13	—we all come in —a perfect man,	—we all attain unto —a fullgrown man,
14	—and cunning craftiness, whereby they lie in wait to deceive;	—in craftiness, after the wiles of error;
16	—fitly joined together and compacted by that	—fitly framed and knit together through that
	—effectual working in the measure of every part,	—working in due measure of each several part,
	—edifying	—building up
17	—that ye henceforth walk not as other Gentiles walk,	—that ye no longer walk as the Gentiles also walk,
18	Having the understanding darkened,	—being darkened in their understanding,
	—blindness	—hardening
22	That ye put off concerning the former conversation the old man, which is corrupt according to the deceitful lusts;	—that ye put away, as concerning your former manner of life, the old man, which waxeth corrupt after the lusts of deceit;
24	—true holiness.	—holiness of truth.
25	—lying,	—falsehood,
28	—that he may have to give to him that needeth.	—that he may have whereof to give to him that hath need.
29	—communication	—speech
	—but that which is good to the use of edifying, that it may minister grace unto the hearers.	—but such as is good for edifying as the need may be, that it may give grace to them that hear.

Chap.	Authorized Version.	Revised Version.
30	—whereby ye are sealed	—in whom ye were sealed
31	—evil speaking,	—railing,
32	—one another,	—each other,
	—God for Christ's sake hath forgiven you.	—God also in Christ forgave you.
5 1	—followers of God, as dear children;	—imitators of God, as beloved children;
2	—for a sweetsmelling savour.	—for an odour of a sweet smell.
3	—be once named	—even be named
4	—convenient:	—befitting:
5	—ye know,	—ye know of a surety,
	—whoremonger,	—fornicator,
6	—vain	—empty
	—children	—sons
8	—sometimes	—once
9	—fruit of the Spirit	—fruit of the light
10	—acceptable	—well-pleasing
11	—reprove	—even reprove
13	—that are	—when they are
	—whatsoever doth make manifest	—every thing that is made manifest
14	—give thee light.	—shine upon thee.
15	See then that ye walk circumspectly, not as fools,	Look therefore carefully how ye walk, not as unwise,
17	—unwise,	—foolish,
	—understanding	—understand
18	—excess;	—riot,
19	—to yourselves	—one to another
20	—unto God and the Father,	—to God, even the Father;

Chap.	Authorized Version.	Revised Version.
21	Submitting —God.	—subjecting —Christ.
22	—submit yourselves	—be in subjection
23	—and he is	—being himself
24	Therefore	But
26	That he might sanctify and cleanse it with the washing of water by the word,	—that he might sanctify it, having cleansed it by the washing of water with the word,
27	—present it	—present the church
29	—the Lord the church:	Christ also the church;
30	—of his flesh, and of his bones.	} *omitted.*
31	—shall be joined unto —they two shall be	—shall cleave to —the twain shall become
32	This is a great mystery: —concerning	This mystery is great: —in regard of
33	Nevertheless let every one of you in particular so love his wife —reverence	Nevertheless do ye also severally love each one his own wife —fear
6 2	—which is the first commandment with promise;	—(which is the first commandment with promise),
4	—but bring them up in the nurture	—but nurture them in the chastening
6	Not with eyeservice,	—not in the way of eyeservice,
8	—any man doeth,	—each one doeth,
9	—knowing that your Master also	—knowing that both their Master and yours

Chap.	Authorized Version.	Revised Version.
10	—my brethren,	*omitted*.
	—power	—strength
12	—we wrestle not	—our wrestling is not
	—against the rulers of the darkness of this world, against spiritual wickedness in high places.	—against the world-rulers of this darkness, against the spiritual hosts of wickedness in the heavenly places.
13	—take unto you	—take up
14	—having your loins girt about with truth, and having on	—having girded your loins with truth, and having put on
15	And your feet shod	—and having shod your feet
16	Above all, taking	—withal taking up
	—the wicked.	—the evil one.
18	Praying always with all prayer and supplication	—with all prayer and supplication praying at all seasons
19	And for me,	—and on my behalf,
	—that I may open my mouth boldly, to make known	—in opening my mouth, to make known with boldness
20	—bonds:	—chains;
	—therein	—in it
22	—for the same purpose,	—for this very purpose,
24	—in sincerity. Amen.	—in uncorruptness.
	¶ Written from Rome unto the Ephesians by Tychicus.	*omitted.*

TO THE PHILIPPIANS.

Chap.		Authorized Version.	Revised Version.
1	1	—Timotheus,	—Timothy,
		—Jesus Christ,	—Christ Jesus,
	2	Grace be unto you,	Grace to you,
		—and the Lord	—and from the Lord
	3	—every remembrance	—all my remembrance
	4	—in every prayer of mine for you all making request	—in every supplication of mine on behalf of you all making my supplication
	5	—in the gospel	—in furtherance of the gospel
	6	—perform	—perfect
	7	—it is meet for me to think this of you all,	—it is right for me to be thus minded on behalf of you all,
		—partakers of my grace.	—partakers with me of grace.
	8	—record,	—witness,
		—bowels	—tender mercies
	9	—judgment;	—discernment;
	12	—I would ye should understand,	—I would have you know,
		—furtherance	—progress
	13	So that my bonds in Christ are manifest in all the palace, and in all other places;	—so that my bonds became manifest in Christ throughout the whole prætorian

Chap.	Authorized Version.	Revised Version.
14	And many of the brethren in the Lord, waxing confident by my bonds, are much more bold to speak the word without fear.	guard, and to all the rest; and that most of the brethren in the Lord, being confident through my bonds, are more abundantly bold to speak the word of God without fear.
16	The one preach Christ of contention, not sincerely, supposing to add affliction to my bonds:	—the one do it of love, knowing that I am set for the defence of the gospel: but the other proclaim Christ of faction, not sincerely, thinking to raise up affliction for me in my bonds.
17	But the other of love, knowing that I am set for the defence of the gospel.	
18	—notwithstanding, every way, —preached;	—only that in every way, —proclaimed;
19	—prayer,	—supplication
20	—I shall be ashamed,	—shall I be put to shame,
22	—this is the fruit	—if this is the fruit
23	—which is far better:	—for it is very far better:
24	Nevertheless —for you.	—yet —for your sake.
25	—and continue with you all for your furtherance and joy of faith;	—yea, and abide with you all, for your progress and joy in the faith; that your glorying may abound in Christ Jesus in me through my presence with you again.
26	That your rejoicing may be more abundant in Jesus Christ for me by my coming to you again.	

Chap.	Authorized Version.	Revised Version.
27	Only let your conversation be as it becometh	Only let your manner of life be worthy of
	—affairs,	—state,
	—mind	—spirit,
28	—terrified by your adversaries:	—affrighted by the adversaries:
29	For unto you it is given	—because to you it hath been granted
	—for his sake;	—in his behalf:
2 1	—consolation	—comfort
	—bowels and mercies,	—tender mercies and compassions,
2	—likeminded,	—of the same mind,
3	—strife	—faction
	—let each esteem other better than themselves.	—each counting other better than himself;
4	Look not every man on his own things, but every man	—not looking each of you to his own things, but each of you
5	Let this mind be in you,	Have this mind in you,
6	—thought it not robbery to be equal with God:	—counted it not a prize to be on an equality with God, but emptied himself,
7	But made himself of no reputation,	
12	Wherefore,	So then,
13	—to do	—to work,
15	—the sons of God, without rebuke,	—children of God without blemish

15

Chap.	Authorized Version.	Revised Version.
15	—ye shine	—ye are seen
16	—I may rejoice	—I may have whereof to glory
18	For the same cause	—and in the same manner
19	—trust	—hope
20	—naturally care	—care truly
22	—as a son with the father,	—as a child serveth a father,
	—in the gospel.	—in furtherance of the gospel.
23	—presently,	—forthwith,
25	Yet I supposed	But I counted
	—companion in labour,	—fellow-worker
	—and he that ministered to my wants.	—and minister to my need;
26	—full of heaviness,	—sore troubled,
28	—carefully,	—diligently,
29	—gladness;	—joy;
	—reputation:	—honour:
30	—not regarding his life,	—hazarding his life
3 1	—grievous,	—irksome,
3	—which worship God in the spirit,	—who worship by the Spirit of God,
	—rejoice	—glory
4	—that he hath whereof he might trust in the flesh, I more:	—to have confidence in the flesh, I yet more:
6	Concerning	—as touching
	—blameless.	—found blameless.
7	But	Howbeit
8	—doubtless,	—verily,

Chap.	Authorized Version.	Revised Version.
8	—but loss —win	—to be loss —gain
9	—mine own righteousness, which is of the law,	—a righteousness of mine own, even that which is of the law,
10	—being made conformable	—becoming conformed
12	—but I follow after, if that I may	—but I press on, if so be that I may
13	—reaching forth	—stretching forward
14	—the mark	—the goal
16	Nevertheless, whereto we have already attained, let us walk by the same rule, let us mind the same thing.	—only, whereunto we have already attained, by that same rule let us walk.
17	—be followers	—be ye imitators
19	—destruction,	—perdition,
20	—look	—wait
21	Who shall change our vile body, that it may be fashioned like unto his glorious body, —subdue	—who shall fashion anew the body of our humiliation, that it may be conformed to the body of his glory, —subject.
4 2	I beseech Euodias, and beseech Syntyche,	I exhort Euodia, and I exhort Syntyche,
3	And I intreat thee —help those women which laboured with me —fellowlabourers,	Yea, I beseech thee —help these women, for they laboured with me —fellow-workers,

Chap.	Authorized Version.	Revised Version.
5	—moderation	—forbearance
6	Be careful for nothing;	In nothing be anxious;
7	—keep your hearts and minds	—guard your hearts and your thoughts
8	—honest,	—honourable,
9	—do:	—these things do:
10	—that now at the last your care for me hath flourished again; wherein ye were also careful,	—that now at length ye have revived your thought for me; wherein ye did indeed take thought,
11	—therewith	—therein
12	—every where	—in every thing
	—I am instructed both to be full and to be hungry, both to abound and to suffer need.	—have I learned the secret both to be filled and to be hungry, both to abound and to be in want.
13	—through Christ which strengtheneth me.	—in him that strengtheneth me.
14	Notwithstanding	Howbeit
	—did communicate	—had fellowship
15	Now ye Philippians know also,	And ye yourselves also know, ye Philippians,
	—communicated	—had fellowship
16	—necessity.	—need.
17	Not because I desire a gift: but I desire fruit that may abound to your account.	Not that I seek for the gift; but I seek for the fruit that increaseth to your account.
19	—shall supply all your need	—shall fulfil every need of yours

Chap.	Authorized Version.	Revised Version.
23	—be with you all. Amen. ¶ It was written to the Philippians from Rome by Epaphroditus.	—be with your spirit. *omitted.*

TO THE COLOSSIANS.

Chap.		Authorized Version.	Revised Version.
1	1	—Jesus Christ	—Christ Jesus
		—Timotheus	—Timothy
	2	—and the Lord Jesus Christ.	} *omitted.*
	4	Since we heard	—having heard
	5	For the hope	—because of the hope
		—in heaven,	—in the heavens,
	6	—as it is in all the world; and bringeth forth fruit,	—even as it is also in all the world bearing fruit and increasing,
	7	—who is for you a faithful minister of Christ;	—who is a faithful minister of Christ on our behalf,
	9	—and to desire	—and make request for you,
	10	—being fruitful	—bearing fruit
	11	Strengthened with all might according to his glorious power,	—strengthened with all power, according to the might of his glory,
		—joyfulness;	—joy;
	13	—his dear Son:	—the Son of his love;
	14	—redemption through his blood,	—our redemption,
	15	—every creature:	—all creation;
	16	—by him, and for him:	—through him, and unto him;

Chap.	Authorized Version.	Revised Version.
19	—it pleased the Father	—it was the good pleasure of the Father
20	And having made peace through the blood of his cross, by him to reconcile all things unto himself;	—and through him to reconcile all things unto himself, having made peace through the blood of his cross;
21	—that were sometime —by wicked works,	—being in time past —in your evil works,
22	—unblameable —in his sight:	—without blemish —before him:
23	If —settled, —to every creature which is under heaven;	—if so be that —stedfast, —in all creation under heaven;
24	Who now rejoice in my sufferings for you, and fill up that which is behind	Now I rejoice in my sufferings for your sake, and fill up on my part that which is lacking
26	—now is made manifest	—now hath it been manifested
27	—would make known	—was pleased to make known
28	Whom we preach, warning every man,	—whom we proclaim, admonishing every man
2 1	For I would that ye knew what great conflict I have for you,	For I would have you know how greatly I strive for you,
2	—to the acknowledg-	—that they may know

Chap.	Authorized Version.	Revised Version.
	ment of the mystery of God, and of the Father, and of Christ;	the mystery of God, even Christ,
4	—lest any man should beguile you with enticing words.	—that no one may delude you with persuasiveness of speech.
7	—abounding therein with thanksgiving.	—abounding in thanksgiving.
8	Beware	Take heed
10	And ye are complete in him,	—and in him ye are made full,
11	—in putting off the body of the sins of the flesh by the circumcision	—in the putting off of the body of the flesh in the circumcision
12	—operation	—working
13	—in your sins	—through your trespasses
	—hath he quickened	—you, I say, did he quicken
14	—the handwriting of ordinances	—the bond written in ordinances
15	And having spoiled	—having put off from himself
16	—an holyday,	—a feast day
18	—beguile you in your reward	—rob you of your prize
	—intruding into those things	—dwelling in the things
19	—holding	—holding fast
	—by joints and bands having nourishment ministered, and knit together	—being supplied and knit together through the joints and bands,

Chap.	Authorized Version.	Revised Version.
20	—are ye subject	—do ye subject yourselves
21	(Touch not; taste not; handle not;	Handle not, nor taste, nor touch (all which things are to perish with the using)
22	Which all are to perish with the using;) —commandments	—precepts
23	—and neglecting of the body; not in any honour to the satisfying of the flesh.	—and severity to the body; but are not of any value against the indulgence of the flesh.
3 1	—be risen with Christ,	—were raised together with Christ,
	—where Christ sitteth	—where Christ is, seated
2	—affection	—mind
3	—ye are dead,	—ye died,
4	—appear,	—be manifested,
5	—inordinate affection, evil concupiscence,	—passion, evil desire,
7	—some time,	—aforetime,
8	—ye also put off all these;	—put ye also away all these;
	—blasphemy, filthy communication	—railing, shameful speaking
9	—deeds;	—doings,
10	—is renewed in knowledge	—is being renewed unto knowledge
11	—there is neither	—there cannot be
	—bond nor free:	—bondman, freeman:
12	—bowels of mercies,	—a heart of compassion,
	—humbleness of mind,	—humility,
13	—quarrel	—complaint

Chap.	Authorized Version.	Revised Version.
13	—Christ	—the Lord
14	—charity,	—love,
15	—God	—Christ
16	—the Lord.	—God.
17	—to God and the Father by him.	—to God the Father through him.
18	Wives, submit yourselves unto your own husbands, as it is fit in the Lord.	Wives, be in subjection to your husbands, as it is fitting in the Lord.
20	—unto the Lord.	—in the Lord.
21	—provoke not your children to anger, lest they be discouraged.	—provoke not your children, that they be not discouraged.
22	—your masters	—them that are your masters
23	—do it heartily,	—work heartily,
24	—reward,	—recompense
4 1	—give	—render
2	Continue in prayer, and watch in the same with thanksgiving;	Continue stedfastly in prayer, watching therein with thanksgiving;
3	—door of utterance,	—door for the word,
6	—every man.	—each one.
7	—state	—affairs
	—declare	—make known
8	—that he might know your estate,	—that ye may know our estate,
10	—Marcus, sister's son to Barnabas,	—Mark the cousin of Barnabas
12	—Christ,	—Christ Jesus,

Chap.	Authorized Version.	Revised Version.
12	—always labouring fervently for you in prayers,	—always striving for you in his prayers,
	—complete	—fully assured
13	—record,	—witness,
	—a great zeal	—much labour
14	—greet	—salute
15	—his house.	—their house.
18	The salutation by the hand of me Paul.	The salutation of me Paul with mine own hand.
	—Amen.	*omitted.*
	¶ Written from Rome to the Colossians by Tychicus and Onesimus.	*omitted.*

I. THESSALONIANS.

Chap.		Authorized Version.	Revised Version.
1	1	—Timotheus,	—Timothy,
		—from God our Father, and the Lord Jesus Christ.	} *omitted.*
	3	—in the sight of God and our Father;	—before our God and Father;
	4	—beloved, your election of God.	—beloved of God, your election,
	5	For our gospel	—how that our gospel
		—we were among you	—we shewed ourselves toward you
	6	—followers	—imitators
	7	—ye were ensamples	—ye became an ensample
	8	—sounded out	—hath sounded forth
		—spread abroad;	—gone forth;
	9	—shew of us	—report concerning us
2	1	—our entrance in unto you, that it was not in vain:	—our entering in unto you, that it hath not been found vain:
	2	But even after that we had suffered before,	—but having suffered before,
		—we were bold	—we waxed bold
		—with much contention.	—in much conflict.
	3	—was not of deceit,	—is not of error,

Chap.	Authorized Version.	Revised Version.
4	But as we were allowed of God to be put in trust with the gospel,	—but even as we have been approved of God to be intrusted with the gospel,
	—trieth	—proveth
5	—used we flattering words,	—were we found using words of flattery,
6	Nor of men sought we glory,	—nor seeking glory of men,
7	—among you,	—in the midst of you,
8	—we were willing to have imparted unto you,	—we were well pleased to impart unto you,
9	—for labouring night and day, because we would not be chargeable unto any of you,	—working night and day, that we might not burden any of you,
10	—justly	—righteously
	—among you	—toward you
11	As ye know how we exhorted and comforted and charged every one of you, as a father doth his children,	—as ye know how we dealt with each one of you, as a father with his own children, exhorting you, and encouraging you, and testifying, to the end that ye should walk worthily of God,
12	That ye would walk worthy of God,	
13	—the word of God which ye heard of us	—from us the word of the message, even the word of God,
	—received	—accepted
	—effectually worketh also	—also worketh

Chap.		Authorized Version.	Revised Version.
	14	—followers	—imitators
		—like things	—the same things
	15	—their own prophets, and have persecuted us;	—the prophets, and drave out us,
	16	—for the wrath	—but the wrath
	17	—being taken from you	—being bereaved of you
		—time	—season
		—abundantly	—exceedingly
	18	Wherefore we would have come unto you,	—because we would fain have come unto you,
	19	—rejoicing?	—glorying?
		—in the presence of	—before
3	1	—left	—left behind
	2	—Timotheus,	—Timothy,
		—and minister of God, and our fellowlabourer in the gospel of Christ,	—and God's minister in the gospel of Christ,
	3	—we are appointed thereunto.	—hereunto we are appointed.
	4	—we told you before that we should suffer tribulation;	—we told you beforehand that we are to suffer affliction;
	6	—good tidings of your faith and charity,	—glad tidings of your faith and love,
		—desiring greatly	—longing
	7	Therefore,	—for this cause,
		—affliction and distress by your faith:	—distress and affliction through your faith:
	9	—thanks	—thanksgiving
	11	Now God himself and	Now may our God and

Chap.	Authorized Version.	Revised Version.
13	our Father, and our Lord Jesus Christ, —before God, even our Father,	Father himself, and our Lord Jesus, —before our God and Father,
4 1	Furthermore —and to please God, so ye would abound	Finally —and to please God, even as ye do walk, —that ye abound
2	—commandments	—charge
4	—every one —possess his vessel	—each one —possess himself of his vessel
5	—lust of concupiscence,	—passion of lust,
6	—go beyond and defraud his brother in any matter:	—transgress, and wrong his brother in the matter:
	—of all such,	—in all these things,
7	—but unto holiness.	—but in sanctification.
8	—despiseth, —who hath also given unto us his Holy Spirit.	—rejecteth, —who giveth his Holy Spirit unto you.
9	But as touching brotherly love ye need not that I write unto you:	But concerning love of the brethren ye have no need that one write unto you.
10	—beseech —increase	—exhort —abound
11	—as we commanded you;	—even as we charged you;
12	—and that ye may have lack of nothing.	—and may have need of nothing.
13	—I would	—we would

Chap.	Authorized Version.	Revised Version.
13	—which are asleep,	—that fall asleep;
	—others	—the rest,
14	—which sleep	—that are fallen asleep
15	—and remain unto the coming of the Lord shall not prevent them which are asleep.	—that are left unto the coming of the Lord, shall in no wise precede them that are fallen asleep.
17	Then we which are alive and remain shall be caught up together with them in the clouds,	—then we that are alive, that are left, shall together with them be caught up in the clouds,
5 1	But of	But concerning
	—that I write unto you.	—that aught be written unto you.
3	For when they shall say,	When they are saying,
	—not	—in no wise
5	—children	—sons
6	Therefore let us not sleep, as do others;	—so then let us not sleep, as do the rest,
8	—who are	—since we are
9	—but to obtain	—but unto the obtaining of
11	—comfort yourselves together, and edify one another,	—exhort one another, and build each other up,
13	—very highly	—exceeding highly
14	Now we exhort you, brethren, warn them that are unruly, comfort the feebleminded, support the weak,	And we exhort you, brethren, admonish the disorderly, encourage the fainthearted, support the

Chap.	Authorized Version.	Revised Version.
	be patient toward all men.	weak, be longsuffering toward all.
15	See that none render evil for evil unto any man; but ever follow that which is good, both among yourselves, and to all men.	See that none render unto any one evil for evil; but alway follow after that which is good, one toward another, and toward all.
16	—evermore.	—alway;
18	—concerning you.	—to you-ward.
22	—all appearance of evil.	—every form of evil.
23	—the very God of peace	—the God of peace himself
	—and I pray God your whole spirit	—and may your spirit
	—be preserved blameless	—be preserved entire, without blame
26	Greet	Salute
27	—charge	—adjure
	—the holy brethren.	—the brethren.
28	—Amen.	*omitted.*
	¶ The first epistle unto the Thessalonians was written from Athens.	*omitted.*

II. THESSALONIANS.

Chap.	Authorized Version.	Revised Version.
1 1	—Timotheus,	—Timothy,
3	—to thank God always	—to give thanks to God alway
	—and the charity of every one of you all toward each other	—and the love of each one of you all toward one another
5	—that ye may	—to the end that ye may
6	Seeing it is	—if so be that it is
	—tribulation	—affliction
	—trouble	—afflict
7	—troubled	—afflicted
	—when the Lord Jesus shall be revealed from heaven with his mighty angels,	—at the revelation of the Lord Jesus from heaven with the angels of his power
8	—taking vengeance on them	—rendering vengeance to them
9	Who shall be punished with everlasting destruction from the presence of the Lord, and from the glory of his power.	—who shall suffer punishment, even eternal destruction from the face of the Lord and from the glory of his might,
10	—admired	—marvelled at
11	Wherefore	To which end
	—all the good pleasure of his goodness,	—every desire of goodness
12	—our Lord Jesus Christ	—our Lord Jesus

Chap.	Authorized Version.	Revised Version.
2 1	—by the coming	—touching the coming
2	That ye be not soon shaken in mind,	—to the end that ye be not quickly shaken from your mind,
	—letter	—epistle
	—the day of Christ is at hand.	—the day of the Lord is now present;
3	Let no man deceive you by any means: for that day shall not come except there come a falling away first,	—let no man beguile you in any wise: for it will not be, except the falling away come first,
4	—he as God sitteth	—he sitteth
	—shewing himself that he is God.	—setting himself forth as God.
6	—what withholdeth that he might be revealed in his time.	—that which restraineth, to the end that he may be revealed in his own season.
7	—iniquity	—lawlessness
	—only he who now letteth will let,	—only there is one that restraineth now,
8	And then shall that Wicked be revealed, whom the Lord shall consume with the spirit of his mouth, and shall destroy with the brightness of his coming:	And then shall be revealed the lawless one, whom the Lord Jesus shall slay with the breath of his mouth, and bring to nought by the manifestation of his coming;
	—after	—according to
10	—deceivableness	—deceit
	—perish;	—are perishing;

Chap.		Authorized Version.	Revised Version.
	11	—God shall send them strong delusion,	—God sendeth them a working of error,
	12	—damned	—judged
	15	—our epistle.	—epistle of ours.
	16	—and God, even our Father,	—and God our Father
		—and hath given us everlasting consolation	—and gave us eternal comfort
	17	—word and work.	—work and word.
3	1	—may have free course,	—may run
	2	—wicked	—evil
	3	—keep you from evil.	—guard you from the evil one.
	5	—patient waiting for Christ.	—patience of Christ.
	6	—he received	—they received
	7	—follow	—imitate
	8	—any man's bread for nought;	—bread for nought at any man's hand,
		—be chargeable to	—burden
	9	—power,	—the right,
		—follow	—imitate
	16	—always by all means.	—at all times in all ways.
	18	—Amen.	*omitted.*
		¶ The second epistle to the Thessalonians was written from Athens.	} *omitted.*

I. TIMOTHY.

Chap.	Authorized Version.	Revised Version.
1 1	Jesus Christ	Christ Jesus
	—and Lord Jesus Christ which is our hope;	—and Christ Jesus our Lord.
2	—my own son in the faith:	—my true child in faith:
3	—Jesus Christ	—Christ Jesus
	As I besought thee to abide still at Ephesus, when I went into Macedonia,	As I exhorted thee to tarry at Ephesus, when I was going into Macedonia,
	—some that they teach no other doctrine,	—certain men not to teach a different doctrine,
4	—which minister questions, rather than godly edifying which is in faith: so do.	—which minister questionings, rather than a dispensation of God, which is in faith; so do I now.
5	—the end of the commandment is charity	—the end of the charge is love
6	—which	—which things
	—jangling;	—talking;
7	—they affirm.	—they confidently affirm.
9	—disobedient,	—unruly,
10	—whoremongers, for them that defile themselves with mankind,	—fornicators, for abusers of themselves with men,

Chap.	Authorized Version.	Revised Version.
10	—perjured persons,	—false swearers,
11	—glorious gospel	—gospel of the glory
12	—Christ Jesus our Lord, who hath enabled me,	—him that enabled me, even Christ Jesus our Lord,
	—putting me into the ministry;	—appointing me to his service;
13	Who was before	—though I was before
14	—was exceeding abundant	—abounded exceedingly
16	—pattern	—ensample
	—life everlasting.	—eternal life.
17	—immortal,	—incorruptible,
	—the only wise God,	—the only God,
18	—son Timothy,	—my child Timothy,
19	—put away concerning faith have made shipwreck:	—thrust from them made shipwreck concerning the faith:
20	—that they may learn	—that they might be taught
2 1	—giving of thanks,	—thanksgivings,
2	—authority;	—high place;
	—a quiet and peaceable life	—a tranquil and quiet life
	—honesty.	—gravity.
4	Who will have all men to be saved,	—who willeth that all men should be saved,
5	—the man Christ Jesus;	—himself man, Christ Jesus,
6	—to be testified in due time.	—the testimony to be borne in its own times;
7	—ordained	—appointed

Chap.	Authorized Version.	Revised Version.
7	—in Christ,	*omitted*.
	—verity.	—truth.
8	I will therefore that men pray everywhere,	I desire therefore that the men pray in every place,
	—doubting.	—disputing.
9	—shamefacedness	—shamefastness
	—broided	—braided
	—array;	—raiment;
10	—with good works.	—through good works.
11	—silence	—quietness
12	—suffer	—permit
	—to usurp authority	—to have dominion
	—silence.	—quietness.
14	—deceived,	—beguiled,
	—was in the transgression.	—hath fallen into transgression:
15	—in childbearing,	—through the childbearing,
	—charity and holiness	—love and sanctification
3 1	This is a true saying,	Faithful is the saying,
	—desire	—seeketh
2	A bishop then must be blameless, the husband of one wife, vigilant, sober, of good behaviour,	The bishop therefore must be without reproach, the husband of one wife, temperate, soberminded, orderly,
3	Not given to wine, no striker, not greedy of filthy lucre; but patient, not a brawler, not covetous	—no brawler, no striker; but gentle, not contentious, no lover of money;

Chap.	Authorized Version.	Revised Version.
6	—lifted up with pride	—puffed up
7	—report	—testimony
8	Likewise must the deacons be grave,	Deacons in like manner must be grave,
10	—then let them use the office of a deacon, being found blameless.	—then let them serve as deacons, if they be blameless.
11	Even so must their wives be grave,	Women in like manner must be grave,
	—sober,	—temperate,
13	—used the office of a deacon well purchase to themselves a good degree,	—served well as deacons gain to themselves a good standing,
15	—how thou oughtest to behave thyself	—how men ought to behave themselves
16	—God was manifest	—He who was manifested
	—unto the Gentiles,	—among the nations,
4 1	—speaketh	—saith
	—depart	—fall away
2	Speaking lies in hypocrisy; having their conscience seared with a hot iron;	—through the hypocrisy of men that speak lies, branded in their own conscience as with a hot iron;
4	—refused,	—rejected,
6	—remembrance	—mind
	—Jesus Christ,	—Christ Jesus,
	—thou hast attained.	—thou hast followed until now:
8	—profiteth little:	—is profitable for a little;

Chap.	Authorized Version.	Revised Version.
9	This is a faithful saying	Faithful is the saying,
10	For therefore we both labour and suffer reproach, because we trust in the living God,	For to this end we labour and strive, because we have our hope set on the living God,
12	—example of the believers, in word, in conversation, in charity, in spirit,	—ensample to them that believe, in word, in manner of life, in love,
13	—attendance	—heed
	—doctrine.	—teaching.
15	Meditate upon these things;	Be diligent in these things;
	—that thy profiting may appear to all.	—that thy progress may be manifest to all.
16	—unto the doctrine;	—to thy teaching.
	—in them:	—in these things;
5 1	—intreat	—exhort
4	—nephews,	—grandchildren,
	—at home,	—towards their own family,
	—for this is good and acceptable before God.	—for this is acceptable in the sight of God.
5	—trusteth in God,	—hath her hope set on God,
6	—liveth in pleasure	—giveth herself to pleasure
7	—give in charge,	—command,
	—blameless.	—without reproach.
8	—those of his own house,	—his own household,
	—infidel.	—unbeliever.

Chap.	Authorized Version.	Revised Version.
9	Let not a widow be taken into the number	Let none be enrolled as a widow
10	—lodged strangers,	—used hospitality to strangers,
11	—they will marry;	—they desire to marry;
12	—damnation,	—condemnation,
	—cast off	—rejected
13	—wandering about	—going about
14	—women	—widows
	—guide the house,	—rule the household,
	—to speak reproachfully.	—for reviling:
16	If any man or woman that believeth have widows, let them relieve them,	If any woman that believeth hath widows, let her relieve them,
	—charged;	—burdened;
17	—doctrine.	—teaching.
18	—reward.	—hire.
19	—but before	—except at the mouth of
20	—rebuke before all,	—reprove in the sight of all,
21	I charge thee before God, and the Lord Jesus Christ,	I charge thee in the sight of God, and Christ Jesus,
	—without preferring one before another,	—without prejudice,
22	—suddenly	—hastily
23	Drink no longer water,	Be no longer a drinker of water,
24	—open beforehand,	—evident,
25	Likewise also the good works of some are	In like manner also there are good works

Chap.	Authorized Version.	Revised Version.
	manifest beforehand; and they that are otherwise cannot be hid.	that are evident; and such as are otherwise cannot be hid.
6 1	—his doctrine	—the doctrine
2	—but rather do them service, because they are faithful and beloved, partakers of the benefit.	—but let them serve them the rather, because they that partake of the benefit are believing and beloved.
3	—teach otherwise, and consent not to wholesome words,	—teacheth a different doctrine, and consenteth not to sound words,
4	—strifes	—disputes
5	Perverse disputings of men of corrupt minds, and destitute of the truth, supposing that gain is godliness:	—wranglings of men corrupted in mind and bereft of the truth, supposing that godliness is a way of gain.
	—from such withdraw thyself.	} omitted.
7	—and it is certain we can carry nothing out.	—for neither can we carry anything out; but having food and covering we shall be therewith content.
8	And having food and raiment let us be therewith content.	
9	—will be rich	—desire to be rich
10	—the root of all evil: which while some coveted after, they have erred from the faith,	—a root of all kinds of evil: which some reaching after have been led astray from the faith,

Chap.	Authorized Version.	Revised Version.
12	—eternal life,	—the life eternal,
	—and hast professed a good profession before many witnesses.	—and didst confess the good confession in the sight of many witnesses.
13	I give thee charge	I charge thee
	—a good confession;	—the good confession;
14	—unrebukeable,	—without reproach,
15	—his times	—its own times
16	—which no man can approach unto;	—unapproachable;
17	—nor trust in uncertain riches, but in the living God,	—nor have their hope set on the uncertainty of riches, but on God,
19	—eternal life.	—the life which is life indeed.
20	—keep that which is committed to thy trust, avoiding profane and vain babblings, and oppositions of science	—guard that which is committed unto thee, turning away from the profane babblings and oppositions of the knowledge
21	—Amen.	*omitted.*
	¶ The first to Timothy was written from Laodicea, which is the chiefest city of Phrygia Pacatiana.	*omitted.*

II. TIMOTHY.

Chap.		Authorized Version.	Revised Version.
1	2	—my dearly beloved son:	—my beloved child:
	3	—that without ceasing I have remembrance of thee in my prayers night and day;	—how unceasing is my remembrance of thee in my supplications, night and day
	4	Greatly desiring to see thee, being mindful of thy tears,	longing to see thee, remembering thy tears,
	5	When I call to remembrance	—having been reminded of
	6	Wherefore	For the which cause
		—by the putting on	—through the laying on
	7	—hath not given us the spirit of fear;	—gave us not a spirit of fearfulness;
		—of a sound mind.	—discipline.
	8	—but be thou partaker of the afflictions of the gospel	—but suffer hardship with the gospel
	9	—before the world began,	—before times eternal,
	10	—immortality	—incorruption
	11	—of the Gentiles.	*omitted.*
	12	—keep (*Also in v.* 14).	—guard
	13	Hold fast the form of	Hold the pattern
	16	—give	—grant

Chap.		Authorized Version.	Revised Version.
2	1	—my son, be strong	—my child, be strengthened
	3	Thou therefore endure hardness,	Suffer hardship with me,
		—Jesus Christ.	—Christ Jesus.
	4	No man that warreth	No soldier on service
		—who hath chosen him to be a soldier.	—who enrolled him as a soldier.
	5	And if a man also strive for masteries, yet he is not crowned, except he strive lawfully.	And if also a man contend in the games, he is not crowned, except he have contended lawfully.
	8	Remember that Jesus Christ of the seed of David was raised from the dead	Remember Jesus Christ, risen from the dead, of the seed of David,
	9	Wherein I suffer trouble, as an evil doer, even unto bonds;	—wherein I suffer hardship unto bonds, as a malefactor;
	11	It is a faithful saying:	Faithful is the saying:
	12	—suffer,	—endure,
	13	—believe not,	—are faithless,
	14	—but to the subverting of the hearers.	—to the subverting of them that hear.
	15	Study to shew thyself	Give diligence to present thyself
		—rightly dividing	—handling aright
	16	—profane and vain babblings:	—profane babblings:
		—increase unto more ungodliness.	—proceed further in ungodliness,
	17	—canker:	—gangrene:
	19	Nevertheless the foun-	Howbeit the firm foun-

Chap.	Authorized Version.	Revised Version.
	dation of God standeth sure,	dation of God standeth,
19	—Christ	—the Lord
	—iniquity.	—unrighteousness.
22	—charity,	—love,
23	—unlearned questions avoid,	—ignorant questionings refuse,
24	—gentle unto all men,	—gentle towards all,
	—patient,	—forbearing,
25	—instructing	—correcting
26	—who are taken captive by him at his will.	—having been taken captive by the Lord's servant unto the will of God.
3 1	This know also,	But know this,
	—perilous	—grievous
2	—covetous, boasters, proud, blasphemers,	—lovers of money, boastful, haughty, railers,
3	—trucebreakers, false accusers, incontinent, fierce, despisers of those that are good,	—implacable, slanderers, without self-control, fierce, no lovers of good, traitors, headstrong, puffed up,
4	Traitors, heady, highminded,	
8	—resist	—withstand
9	—manifest	—evident
	—their's also was.	—theirs also came to be.
10	But thou hast fully known my doctrine, manner of life,	But thou didst follow my teaching, conduct
	—charity,	—love,

Chap.	Authorized Version.	Revised Version.
11	—afflictions, which came upon me	—sufferings; what things befel me
13	—seducers	—impostors
14	—continue	—abide
15	—from a child thou hast known the holy scriptures,	—from a babe thou hast known the sacred writings,
16	All scripture is given by inspiration of God, and is profitable for doctrine,	Every scripture inspired of God is also profitable for teaching,
17	—perfect, thoroughly furnished	—complete, furnished completely
4 1	I charge thee therefore before God, and the Lord Jesus Christ,	I charge thee in the sight of God, and of Christ Jesus,
	—at his appearing	—and by his appearing
2	—doctrine.	—teaching.
5	—watch thou	—be thou sober
	—endure afflictions,	—suffer hardship,
	—make full proof of thy ministry.	—fulfil thy ministry.
6	—now ready to be offered,	—already being offered,
	—is at hand.	—is come.
8	—that love	—that have loved
10	—and is departed unto	—and went to
11	—he is profitable to me for the ministry.	—he is useful to me for ministering.
14	—reward him	—will render to him
16	At my first answer no man stood with me, but all men forsook	At my first defence no one took my part, but all forsook me:

Chap.	Authorized Version.	Revised Version.
	me: I pray God that it may not be laid to their charge.	may it not be laid to their account.
17	Notwithstanding the Lord stood with me,	But the Lord stood by me,
	—the preaching might be fully known,	—the message might be fully proclaimed,
18	—preserve	—save
19	—household	—house
21	—greeteth	—saluteth
22	The Lord Jesus Christ	The Lord
	—Amen.	*omitted.*
	¶ The second epistle unto Timotheus, ordained the first bishop of the church of the Ephesians, was written from Rome, when Paul was brought before Nero the second time.	*omitted.*

TO TITUS.

Chap.		Authorized Version.	Revised Version.
1	1	—acknowledging	—knowledge
		—after godliness;	—according to godliness;
	2	—before the world began;	—before times eternal;
	3	But hath in due times manifested his word through preaching, which is committed unto me	—but in his own seasons manifested his word in the message, wherewith I was intrusted
	4	—mine own son	—my true child
		—Grace, mercy, and peace,	—Grace and peace
		—the Lord Jesus Christ	—Christ Jesus
	5	—ordain elders in every city, as I had appointed thee:	—appoint elders in every city, as I gave thee charge;
	6	If any be	—if any man is
		—faithful children	—children that believe,
	7	—not given to wine,	—no brawler,
		—not given to	—not greedy of
	8	—a lover of	—given to
		—sober,	—sober-minded,
	9	Holding fast	—holding to
		—as he hath been taught,	—which is according to the teaching,
		—convince	—convict

Chap.		Authorized Version.	Revised Version.
	11	—who subvert whole houses,	—men who overthrow whole houses,
	12	—slow bellies.	—idle gluttons.
	13	—witness	—testimony
		—Wherefore rebuke them	For which cause reprove them
	16	—in works	—by their works
2	1	—become	—befit
	2	—sober, grave, temperate,	—temperate, grave, soberminded,
		—in charity,	—in love,
	3	—that they be in behaviour as becometh holiness, not false accusers, not given to much wine, teachers of good things;	—be reverent in demeanour, not slanderers nor enslaved to much wine, teachers of that which is good;
	4	—teach	—train
		—to be sober, to love their husbands, to love their children,	—to love their husbands, to love their children, to be soberminded,
	5	To be discreet, chaste, keepers at home, good, obedient to their own husbands,	chaste, workers at home, kind, being in subjection to their own husbands,
	6	Young men	—the younger men
	7	—a pattern	—an ensample
		—sincerity.	*omitted.*
	9	—obedient	—in subjection
		—to please them well	—to be well-pleasing to them
		—answering again;	—gainsaying;

Chap.	Authorized Version.	Revised Version.
12	Teaching us that,	—instructing us, to the intent that,
13	—the glorious appearing	—appearing of the glory
14	—a peculiar people,	—a people for his own possession,
15	—rebuke	—reprove
3 1	—to be subject to principalities and powers, to obey magistrates,	—to be in subjection to rulers, to authorities, to be obedient,
2	—to be no brawlers, but gentle,	—not to be contentious, to be gentle,
3	—sometimes	—aforetime
4	But after that	But when
5	Not by works of righteousness which we have done,	—not by works done in righteousness, which we did ourselves,
6	Which he shed on us abundantly	—which he poured out upon us richly,
8	This is a faithful saying, and these things I will that thou affirm constantly, that they which have believed	Faithful is the saying, and concerning these things I will that thou affirm confidently, to the end that they which have believed
9	—avoid foolish questions,	—shun foolish questionings,
	—contentions,	—strifes,
	—strivings	—fightings
10	—an heretick	—heretical
	—reject;	—refuse;
11	—subverted,	—perverted,
	—condemned of himself.	—self-condemned,

Chap.	Authorized Version.	Revised Version.
12	—be diligent	—give diligence
13	Bring	Set forward
14	—our's	—our people
15	—Greet	Salute
	—Amen.	*omitted.*
	¶ It was written to Titus, ordained the first bishop of the church of the Cretians, from Nicapolis of Macedonia.	*omitted.*

TO PHILEMON.

Chap.	Authorized Version.	Revised Version.
1	—Jesus Christ,	—Christ Jesus,
	—our dearly beloved, and fellow-labourer,	—our beloved and fellow-worker,
2	—to our beloved Apphia,	—to Apphia our sister,
6	—communication	—fellowship
	—by the acknowledging	—in the knowledge
	—in Christ Jesus.	—unto Christ.
7	For we had great joy and consolation in thy love,	For I had much joy and comfort in thy love,
	—bowels	—hearts
8	—I might be much bold	—I have all boldness
	—convenient,	—befitting,
9	—Jesus Christ.	—Christ Jesus:
10	—son	—child,
11	Which in time past was to thee unprofitable,	—who was aforetime unprofitable to thee,
12	Whom I have sent again: thou therefore receive him, that is, mine own bowels:	—whom I have sent back to thee in his own person, that is, my very heart:
13	—I would have retained	—I would fain have kept
	—stead	—behalf
14	—benefit	—goodness

Chap.	Authorized Version.	Revised Version.
14	—willingly.	—of free will.
15	—he therefore departed	—he was therefore parted
	—receive him	—have him
16	Not now	—no longer
	—above	—more than
19	—albeit I do not say	—that I say not
20	—refresh my bowels in the Lord.	—refresh my heart in Christ.
21	—more than I say.	—even beyond what I say.
22	—trust	—hope
	—given	—granted
24	Marcus, Aristarchus, Demas, Lucas, my fellow-labourers.	—and so do Mark, Aristarchus, Demas, Luke, my fellow-workers.
	¶ Written from Rome to Philemon by Onesimus a servant.	} *omitted.*

TO THE HEBREWS.

Chap.	Authorized Version.	Revised Version.
1 1	God, who at sundry times, and in divers manners spake in time past unto the fathers by the prophets,	God, having of old time spoken unto the fathers in the prophets by divers portions and in divers manners, hath
2	Hath in these last days	at the end of these days
3	—brightness	—effulgence
	—express image of his person,	—very image of his substance,
	—by himself purged our sins,	—made purification of sins,
4	Being made so much better	—having become by so much better
6	—first begotten	—firstborn
7	—spirits,	—winds,
8	—righteousness	—uprightness
11	—thou remainest;	—thou continuest:
12	—vesture	—mantle
	—fold them up,	—roll them up, As a garment,
13	—thy footstool?	—the footstool of thy feet?
14	—to minister for them who shall be heirs of salvation?	—to do service for the sake of them that shall inherit salvation?

Chap.		Authorized Version.	Revised Version.
2	1	—which we have heard, lest at any time we should let them slip.	—that were heard, lest haply we drift away from them.
	2	—by angels was stedfast,	—through angels proved stedfast,
	4	—with divers miracles,	—by manifold powers,
	5	For unto the angels hath he not put in subjection	—For not unto angels did he subject
	6	—in a certain place	—hath somewhere
	8	—put under him.	—subject to him.
	9	But we see Jesus, who was made a little lower than the angels for the suffering of death,	But we behold him who hath been made a little lower than the angels, even Jesus, because of the suffering of death
	10	—captain	—author
	12	—in the midst of the church will I sing praise unto thee.	In the midst of the congregation will I sing thy praise.
	14	—partakers of	—sharers in
		—likewise took part	—in like manner partook
		—destroy	—bring to nought
	16	For verily he took not on him the nature of angels; but he took on him the seed of Abraham.	For verily not of angels doth he take hold, but he taketh hold of the seed of Abraham.
	17	—reconciliation	—propitiation
3	1	—the heavenly calling,	—a heavenly calling,
		—of our profession, Christ Jesus;	—of our confession, even Jesus;
	3	—this man was counted	—he hath been counted

P.	Authorized Version.	Revised Version.
4	—some man;	—some one;
5	—verily	—indeed
	—to be spoken after;	—afterward to be spoken;
6	—the confidence and the rejoicing	—our boldness and the glorying
8	—in the day of temptation	Like as in the day of the temptation
9	When your fathers tempted me, proved me,	Wherewith your fathers tempted me by proving me,
10	—grieved with that generation,	—displeased with this generation,
	—and they have not known	But they did not know
11	So	As
12	—lest there be	—lest haply there shall be
	—departing	—falling away
13	—daily, while	—day by day, so long as
14	—stedfast	—firm
16	For some,	For who,
	—howbeit not all that came out of Egypt by Moses.	—nay, did not all they that came out of Egypt by Moses?
17	—grieved	—displeased
18	—that believed not?	—that were disobedient?
19	So we see that they could not enter	And we see that they were not able to enter
1	—lest,	—lest haply,
2	For unto us was the gospel preached, as well as unto them: but the word preach-	For indeed we have had good tidings preached unto us, even as also they:

Chap.	Authorized Version.	Revised Version.
	ed did not profit them, not being mixed with faith in them that heard it.	but the word of hearing did not profit them, because they were not united by faith with them that heard.
3	—if they shall enter into my rest:	They shall not enter into my rest:
4	For he spake in a certain place	For he hath said somewhere
5	—If they shall enter into my rest.	They shall not enter into my rest.
6	—it was first preached entered not in because of unbelief:	—the good tidings were before preached failed to enter in because of disobedience,
7	Again, he limiteth a certain day,	—he again defineth a certain day,
	—as it is said,	—as it hath been before said
8	—Jesus	—Joshua
9	—a rest	—a sabbath rest
10	—he also hath ceased	—hath himself also rested
11	—labour therefore	—therefore give diligence
	—lest any man fall	—that no man fall
	—unbelief.	—disobedience.
12	—quick, and powerful,	—living, and active,
	—and is a discerner of	—and quick to discern
13	—opened unto	—laid open before
14	Seeing then that we have	—Having then

Chap.	Authorized Version.	Revised Version.
14	—profession.	—confession.
15	—but was	—but one that hath been
16	—come boldly	—draw near with boldness
	—obtain	—receive
5 1	—ordained	—appointed
2	Who can have compassion on the ignorant, and on them that are out of the way;	—who can bear gently with the ignorant and erring,
3	—he ought,	—is bound,
4	—but he that is called of God,	—but when he is called of God,
5	—said	—spake
7	—in that he feared;	—for his godly fear,
10	Called	—named
11	—hard to be uttered,	—hard of interpretation,
12	—for the time	—by reason of the time
	—which be the first principles	—the rudiments of the first principles
	—strong meat.	—solid food.
13	—useth	—partaketh of
	—unskilful	—without experience
14	But strong meat belongeth to them that are of full age,	But solid food is for fullgrown men,
6 1	Therefore leaving the principles of the doctrine of Christ, let us go on	Wherefore let us cease to speak of the first principles of Christ, and press on
2	—doctrine	—teaching

Chap.	Authorized Version.	Revised Version.
5	—the world to come,	—the age to come,
6	If they shall fall away,	—and then fell away,
7	—the earth which drinketh in	—the land which hath drunk
	—by whom it is dressed,	—for whose sake it is also tilled,
8	But that which beareth thorns and briars is rejected, and is nigh unto cursing;	—but if it beareth thorns and thistles, it is rejected and nigh unto a curse;
10	—labour of love,	—the love
	—and do	—and still do
11	—to the full assurance of hope unto the end:	—unto the fulness of hope even to the end:
12	—not slothful, but followers	—not sluggish, but imitators
13	—because	—since
15	And so, after he had	—And thus, having
16	—men verily swear	—men swear
	—and an oath for confirmation is to them an end of all strife.	—and in every dispute of theirs the oath is final for confirmation.
17	—willing	—being minded
	—confirmed it by	—interposed with
18	—consolation,	—encouragement,
7 1	—priest of the most high God,	—priest of God Most High,
2	—gave	—divided
3	—descent,	—genealogy,
4	—a tenth of the spoils.	—a tenth out of the chief spoils.

Chap.	Authorized Version.	Revised Version.
5	And verily they that are	And they indeed
	—office of the priesthood,	—priest's office
6	—descent	—genealogy
	—received	—hath taken
7	—without all contradiction	—without any dispute
8	—but there he receiveth them	—but there one,
9	And as I may so say, Levi also, who receiveth tithes, payed tithes in Abraham.	And, so to say, through Abraham even Levi, who receiveth tithes, hath paid tithes;
11	If therefore perfection were by	Now if there was perfection through
	—called	—reckoned
13	—spoken pertaineth	—said belongeth
14	—of which tribe	—as to which tribe
	—priesthood.	—priests.
15	And it is yet far more evident: for that after the similitude of Melchisedec	And what we say is yet more abundantly evident, if after the likeness of Melchizedek
17	For he testifieth,	—for it is witnessed of him,
18	—there is verily	—there is
	—the commandment going before for the weakness and unprofitableness thereof.	—a foregoing commandment because of its weakness and unprofitableness
19	—but the bringing in of	—and a bringing in there-

Chap.	Authorized Version.	Revised Version.
	a better hope did; by the which we draw nigh unto God.	upon of a better hope, through which we draw nigh unto God.
20	—as not without an oath he was made priest:	—as it is not without the taking of an oath
21	(For those priests were made	—(for they indeed have been made priests
	—repent,	—repent himself,
	—after the order of Melchisedec:)	} *omitted.*
22	—testament.	—covenant.
23	And they truly were many priests, because they were not suffered to continue by reason of death:	And they indeed have been made priests many in number, because that by death they are hindered from continuing:
24	But this man, because he continueth ever, hath an unchangeable priesthood.	but he, because he abideth for ever, hath his priesthood unchangeable.
25	—that come unto God by him,	—that draw near unto God through him,
26	—who is holy, harmless,	—holy, guileless,
	—separate	—separated
27	—the people's:	—the sins of the people:
	—once,	—once for all,
28	—maketh	—appointeth
	—since	—after
	—maketh the Son, who is consecrated for evermore.	—appointeth a Son, perfected for evermore.

Chap.	Authorized Version.	Revised Version.
8 1	Now of the things which we have spoken this is the sum:	Now in the things which we are saying the chief point is this:
	—who is set	—who sat down
3	—ordained	—appointed
4	—he should not be a priest,	—he would not be a priest at all,
	—there are priests	—there are those
5	—unto the example	—that which is a copy
	—was admonished	—is warned
6	—a more excellent ministry,	—a ministry the more excellent,
	—was established	—hath been enacted
11	—neighbour,	—fellow-citizen,
12	—unrighteousness,	—iniquities,
	—and their iniquities	*omitted.*
13	—Now that which decayeth and waxeth old is ready to vanish away.	But that which is becoming old and waxeth aged is nigh unto vanishing away.
9 1	Then verily	Now even
	—and a worldly sanctuary.	—and its sanctuary, a sanctuary of this world.
2	—made;	—prepared,
	—the sanctuary.	—the Holy place.
3	—the Holiest of all;	—the Holy of holies;
4	—the golden pot that had manna,	—a golden pot holding the manna,
5	—particularly.	—severally.
6	—were thus ordained,	—having been thus pre-

Chap.	Authorized Version.	Revised Version.
	the priests went always into the first tabernacle, accomplishing the service of God.	pared, the priests go in continually into the first tabernacle, accomplishing the services;
8	—the holiest of all	—the holy place
9	—was a figure	—is a parable
	—that could not make him that did the service perfect, as pertaining to the conscience;	—that cannot, as touching the conscience, make the worshipper perfect, being only (with meats and drinks and divers washings) carnal ordinances,
10	Which stood only in meats and drinks, and divers washings, and carnal ordinances,	
11	—building;	—creation,
12	Neither by	—nor yet through
	—once	—once for all
	—for us.	*omitted.*
13	—the unclean,	—them that have been defiled,
	—purifying	—cleanness
14	—spot	—blemish
	—purge	—cleanse
15	—the new testament, that by means of death,	—a new covenant, that a death having taken place
	—the first testament,	—the first covenant,
16	—the testator.	—him that made it.
17	—after men are dead: otherwise it is of no strength at all while the testator liveth.	—where there hath been death: for doth it ever avail while he that made it liveth?

18

Chap.	Authorized Version.	Revised Version.
18	Whereupon neither the first testament was dedicated without blood.	Wherefore even the first covenant hath not been dedicated without blood.
19	—precept	—commandment
20	—of the testament which God hath enjoined unto you.	—of the covenant which God commanded to you-ward.
22	And almost all things are by the law purged with blood; and without	And according to the law, I may almost say, all things are cleansed with blood, and apart from
23	—patterns	—copies
	—purified	—cleansed
24	—which are the figures of the true;	—like in pattern to the true;
	—in the presence of	—before the face of
25	—every year with the blood of others;	—year by year with blood not his own;
26	For then	—else
	—but now once in the end of the world hath he appeared	—but now once at the end of the ages hath he been manifested
27	And as	And inasmuch as
	—after this	—after this cometh
28	—look	—wait
	—without sin	—apart from sin,
10 1	—make the comers thereunto perfect.	—make perfect them that draw nigh.
2	For then	Else
	—once purged	—having been once cleansed,

Chap.	Authorized Version.	Revised Version.
3	—again made of sins every year.	—made of sins year by year.
6	—burnt offerings	—whole burnt offerings
7	—volume	—roll
8	Above when he said,	Saying above,
	—offering for sin	—sacrifices for sin
	—which are offered by the law;	—(the which are offered according to the law)
9	Then said he,	—then hath he said,
11	—daily	—day by day
12	But this man,	—but he,
13	—his footstool.	—the footstool of his feet.
15	Whereof the Holy Ghost also is a witness to us: for after that he had said before,	And the Holy Ghost also beareth witness to us: for after he hath said,
17	And their sins	—then saith he, And their sins
20	By a new and living way, which he hath consecrated for us,	—by the way which he dedicated for us, a new and living way,
21	—an high priest	—a great priest
22	—full assurance	—-fulness
23	—the profession of our faith without wavering;	—the confession of our hope that it waver not;
25	—manner	—custom
	—approaching.	—drawing nigh.
27	—looking for	—expectation
	—fiery indignation,	—a fierceness of fire

Chap.	Authorized Version.	Revised Version.
28	He that despised Moses' law	A man that hath set at nought Moses' law
	—under	—on the word of
29	—suppose	—think
	—thought	—judged
30	—saith the Lord.	*omitted.*
32	—illuminated,	—enlightened,
	—fight of afflictions;	—conflict of sufferings;
33	—companions of	—partakers with
34	—on me in my bonds,	—on them that were in bonds,
	—goods, knowing in yourselves that ye have in heaven a better and an enduring substance.	—possessions, knowing that ye yourselves have a better possession and an abiding one.
35	—confidence,	—boldness,
38	Now the just	But my righteous one
	—but if any man draw back,	And if he shrink back,
39	—who draw back	—that shrink back
	—that believe	—that have faith
1	—substance	—assurance
	—evidence	—proving
2	For by it the elders obtained a good report.	For therein the elders had witness borne to them.
4	—by which he obtained witness	—through which he had witness borne to him
	—God testifying to his gifts:	—God bearing witness in respect of his gifts:

Chap.	Authorized Version.	Revised Version.
5	—he had this testimony, that he pleased God.	—he hath had witness borne to him that he had been well-pleasing unto God:
6	—to please him:	—to be well-pleasing unto him:
	—diligently seek him.	—seek after him.
7	—moved with fear,	—moved with godly fear,
	—by faith.	—according to faith.
8	—to go out	—obeyed to go out
9	—he sojourned	—he became a sojourner
	—a strange country,	—a land not his own,
	—tabernacles	—tents,
11	—strength	—power
	—because she judged	—since she counted
12	—sky	—heaven
13	—having seen them afar off,	—having seen them and greeted them from afar,
	—and were persuaded of them, and embraced them,	} *omitted.*
14	—declare plainly that they seek a country.	—make it manifest that they are seeking after a country of their own.
17	—had received	—had gladly received
18	Of whom it was said,	—even he to whom it was said,
19	—from whence also he received him in a figure.	—from whence he did also in a parable receive him back.
21	—both the sons	—each of the sons
22	—when he died,	—when his end was nigh,

Chap.	Authorized Version.	Revised Version.
23	—proper	—goodly
24	—come to years,	—grown up,
25	—to suffer affliction	—to be evil entreated
26	Esteeming	—accounting
	—he had respect	—he looked
28	—he that destroyed	—the destroyer of
29	—drowned.	—swallowed up.
31	—believed not,	—were disobedient,
34	—violence	—power
	—valiant in fight,	—mighty in war,
35	—raised to life again:	—by a resurrection:
37	—wandered	—went
	—tormented;	—evil entreated
38	—in dens and caves of the earth.	—and caves, and the holes of the earth.
39	—obtained a good report	—had witness borne to them
40	—that they without us	—that apart from us they
12 2	—finisher	—perfecter
	—is set down	—hath sat down
3	—contradiction of sinners against himself, lest ye be wearied and faint in your minds.	—gainsaying of sinners against themselves, that ye wax not weary, fainting in your souls.
5	—which speaketh unto you as unto children,	—which reasoneth with you as with sons,
	—despise not thou	—regard not lightly
	—rebuked	—reproved
7	If ye endure chastening,	It is for chastening that ye endure;
9	—which corrected us,	—to chasten us,

Chap.	Authorized Version.	Revised Version.
10	—after their own pleasure;	—as seemed good to them;
11	—peaceable fruit of righteousness	—peaceable fruit
12	—feeble	—palsied
13	—but let it rather	—but rather
14	—holiness,	—the sanctification
15	—diligently lest any man fail	—carefully lest there be any man that falleth short
	—many	—the many
16	—morsel	—mess
17	—how that afterward, when he would have inherited the blessing, he was rejected: for he found no place of repentance, though he sought it	—that even when he afterward desired to inherit the blessing, he was rejected (for he found no place of repentance), though he sought it
19	—spoken to them any more:	—spoken unto them:
20	—commanded,	—enjoined,
	—or thrust through with a dart:	} omitted.
21	—so terrible was the sight,	—so fearful was the appearance,
22	—company	—hosts
23	—written	—enrolled
25	—who refused him that spake on earth,	—when they refused him that warned them on earth,
	—if we turn away from him that speaketh from heaven:	—who turn away from him that warneth from heaven:

Chap.	Authorized Version.	Revised Version.
26	—I shake not the earth only,	—will I make to tremble not the earth only,
28	—moved,	—shaken,
	—we may serve God acceptably with reverence and godly fear:	—we may offer service well-pleasing to God with reverence and awe:
13 1	—brotherly love	—love of the brethren
2	Be not forgetful to entertain strangers:	Forget not to shew love unto strangers:
3	—them which suffer adversity,	—them that are evil entreated,
4	Marriage is honourable in all, and the bed undefiled: but whoremongers	Let marriage be had in honour among all, and let the bed be undefiled: for fornicators
5	Let your conversation be without covetousness; and be content with such things as ye have: for he hath said, I will never leave thee, nor forsake thee.	Be ye free from the love of money; content with such things as ye have: for himself hath said, I will in no wise fail thee, neither will I in any wise forsake thee.
6	So that we may boldly say,	So that with good courage we say,
7	—which have the rule	—that had the rule
	—whose faith follow, considering the end of their conversation:	—and considering the issue of their life, imitate their faith.
8	—the same	—is the same
	—and for ever.	—yea and for ever.

Chap.	Authorized Version.	Revised Version.
9	—doctrines.	—teachings:
	—established	—stablished
	—which have not profited them that have been occupied therein.	—wherein they that occupied themselves were not profited.
11	—the sanctuary	—the holy place
	—for sin,	—as an offering for sin,
14	For here have we no continuing city, but we seek one to come.	For we have not here an abiding city, but we seek after the city which is to come.
15	—giving thanks	—which make confession
17	—submit yourselves:	—submit to them:
	—for your souls,	—in behalf of your souls,
18	—we trust	—we are persuaded that
	—in all things willing to live honestly.	—desiring to live honestly in all things.
19	But I beseech you the rather to do this,	And I exhort you the more exceedingly to do this,
20	—our Lord Jesus, that great Shepherd of the sheep, through the blood of the everlasting covenant.	—the great shepherd of the sheep with the blood of the eternal covenant, even our Lord Jesus,
21	—work	—thing
	—working in you	—working in us
22	—beseech	—exhort
	—suffer	—bear with
	—written a letter	—written
	¶ Written to the Hebrews from Italy by Timothy.	} *omitted.*

JAMES.

Various readings followed
A.V. added here. *Westcott & Hort's*
omit added here

CHAP.		AUTHORIZED VERSION.	REVISED VERSION.
1	1	—scattered abroad,	of the Dispersion,
	2	—divers	—manifold
	3	—trying	—proof
	4	—*her* perfect work,	—its perfect work,
		—wanting nothing.	—lacking in nothing.
	5	—to all *men*	—to all
	6	—wavering.	—doubting:
		—wavereth	—doubteth
		—wave	—surge
	8	A double minded man is unstable	—a doubleminded man, unstable
	9	—rejoice in that he is exalted:	—glory in his high estate:
	11	—is no sooner risen with a burning heat,	—ariseth with the scorching wind,
		—ways.	—goings.
	12	—he is tried,	—he hath been approved,
	13	—neither tempteth he any man:	—and he himself tempteth no man:
	14	—every man	—each man
	15	—when it is finished,	—when it is full-grown
	16	Do not err,	Be not deceived,
	17	—perfect gift	—perfect boon
		—with whom is no variableness, neither shadow of turning.	—with whom can be no variation, neither shadow that is cast by turning.

Chap.	Authorized Version.	Revised Version.
18	—begat he us	—he brought us forth
19	Wherefore my beloved brethren, let every man	Ye know this, my beloved brethren. But let every man
21	—lay apart all filthiness and superfluity of naughtiness,	—putting away all filthiness and overflowing of wickedness,
	—engrafted	—implanted
22	—deceiving	—deluding
23	—a glass:	—a mirror
25	But whoso looketh into the perfect law of liberty, and continueth [therein] he being not a forgetful hearer, but a doer of the work,	But he that looketh into the perfect law, the law of liberty, and [so] continueth, being not a hearer that forgetteth, but a doer that worketh,
25	—deed.	—doing.
26	If any man among you seem to be religious,	If any man thinketh himself to be religious,
2 1	—have not	—hold not
2	—assembly	—synagogue
	—goodly apparel,	—fine clothing;
	—raiment;	—clothing;
3	—respect	—regard
	—gay	—fine
4	Are ye not then partial in yourselves, and are become judges of evil thoughts?	—are ye not divided in your own mind, and become judges with evil thoughts?
6	—despised the poor.	—dishonoured the poor man.

Chap.	Authorized Version.	Revised Version.
6	—and draw you	—and themselves drag you
7	—that worthy name	—the honourable name
9	—convinced of the law	—convicted by the law
10	—offend	—stumble
12	—by the law	—by a law
13	For he shall have judgment without mercy,	For judgement is without mercy to him
	—rejoiceth	—glorieth
15	—destitute	—in lack
16	—Depart	—Go
17	—is dead, being alone.	—is dead in itself.
18	—without	—apart from
	—and I will shew thee my faith by my works.	—and I by my works will shew thee my faith.
19	—there is one God ;	—God is one ;
	—tremble.	—shudder.
20	—without works is dead ?	—apart from works is barren ?
21	—when he had offered	—in that he offered
22	Seest thou..	Thou seest
23	—imputed	—reckoned
	—the Friend of God.	—the friend of God.
25	Likewise also	And in like manner
26	—without	—apart from
3 1	—masters,	—teachers,
	—the greater condemnation.	—heavier judgment.
2	—offend all.	—all stumble.
	—offend not	—stumbleth not

Chap.	Authorized Version.	Revised Version.
3	Behold, we put bits in the horses' mouths,	Now if we put the horses' bridles into their mouths,
4	—of fierce	—by rough
	—helm, whithersoever the governor listeth.	—rudder, whither the impulse of the steersman willeth.
5	—how great a matter a little fire kindleth!	—how much wood is kindled by how small a fire!
6	—a world of iniquity: so is the tongue among our members,	—the world of iniquity among our members is the tongue,
6	—the course of nature;	—the wheel of nature,
7	—serpents,	—creeping things
9	—God, even the Father;	—the Lord and Father;
	—similitude	—likeness
10	—proceedeth	—cometh forth
11	—at the same place	—from the same opening
12	—bear olive berries?	—yield olives,
	—so can no fountain both yield salt water and fresh.	—neither can salt water yield sweet.
13	—endued with knowledge	—understanding
	—out of a good conversation	—by his good life
14	—envying and strife	—jealousy and faction
15	—descendeth not from above,	—is not a wisdom that cometh down from above,
16	—where envying and strife is,	—jealousy and faction are,

Chap.	Authorized Version.	Revised Version.
16	—evil work.	—vile deed.
17	—partiality,	—variance,
18	—of them	—for them
4 1	—lusts	—pleasures
2	—desire to have,	—covet,
3	—consume it upon your lusts.	—spend it in your pleasures.
4	Ye adulterers and adulteresses,	Ye adulteresses,
	—is the enemy	—maketh himself an enemy
5	Do ye think that the scripture saith in vain, The spirit that dwelleth in us lusteth to envy?	Or think ye that the scripture speaketh in vain? Doth the spirit which he made to dwell in us long unto envying?
6	—he saith,	—the scripture saith,
7	Submit yourselves	Be subject
	—Resist	—but resist
10	—lift you us.	—exalt you.
11	Speak not evil one of another,	Speak not one against another,
	—speaketh evil of	—speaketh against.
12	There is one lawgiver, who is able	One only is the lawgiver and judge, even he who is able
	—another?	—thy neighbour?
13	—and continue there a year, and buy and sell,	—and spend a year there, and trade,
14	—It is even a vapour,	For ye are a vapour,

Chap.		Authorized Version.	Revised Version.
	16	—rejoice in your boastings :	—glory in your vauntings :
		—rejoicing	—glorying
5	1	—that shall come	—that are coming
	3	—cankered ;	—rusted ;
		—witness	—testimony
		—Ye have heaped treasure together for the last days.	—Ye have laid up your treasure in the last days.
	4	—have reaped down	—mowed
		—sabaoth.	Sabaoth.
	5	—in pleasure	—delicately
		—been wanton ;	—taken your pleasure ;
	6	—the just ;	—the righteous one ;
	7	—and hath long patience for it,	—being patient over it,
	8	—draweth nigh.	—is at hand.
	9	Grudge	Murmur
		—lest ye be condemned :	—that ye be not judged :
	10	—suffering affliction,	—suffering
	11	Behold, we count them happy which endure.	Behold, we call them blessed which endured :
		—very pitiful, and of tender mercy.	—full of pity, and merciful.
	12	—lest ye fall into condemnation.	—that ye fall not under judgement.
	13	—afflicted ?	—suffering ?
		—merry ?	—cheerful ?
		—psalms.	—praise.
	16	Confess your faults one to another,	Confess therefore your sins one to another,

Chap.	Authorized Version.	Revised Version.
16	The effectual fervent prayer of a righteous man availeth much.	The supplication of a righteous man availeth much in its working.
17	Elias	Elijah
	—subject to like passions	—of like passions
	—earnestly	—fervently
	—by the space of	—for
20	—hide	—cover

I. PETER.

Chap.		Authorized Version.	Revised Version.
1	1	—to the strangers scattered throughout	—to the elect who are sojourners of the Dispersion in
	3	—abundant	—great
		—lively	—living
	5	—kept	—guarded
	6	—a season,	—a little while,
		—ye are in heaviness	—ye have been put to grief
	7	—trial	—proof
		—tried	—proved
		—appearing	—revelation
	8	—ye rejoice	—ye rejoice greatly
	10	Of which	Concerning which
		—have enquired	—sought
	11	—signify,	—point unto,
	12	—reported	—announced
	13	—hope to the end for the grace	—set your hope perfectly on the grace
	14	As obedient children,	—as children of obedience,
		—in your ignorance:	—in the time of your ignorance:
	15	But as he	—but like as he
		—conversation;	—living;

Chap.	Authorized Version.	Revised Version.
17	—on the Father,	—on him as Father,
18	Forasmuch as ye know that ye were not redeemed with corruptible things,	—knowing that ye were redeemed, not with corruptible things,
	—vain conversation received by tradition	—vain manner of life handed down
19	But with the precious blood of Christ, as a lamb without blemish and without spot:	—but with precious blood, as of a lamb without blemish and without spot, even the blood of Christ:
20	Who verily was foreordained	—who was foreknown indeed
	—manifest in these last times for you,	—manifested at the end of the times for your sake,
21	Who by him do believe in God,	—who through him are believers in God,
22	—in obeying	—in your obedience to
	—see that ye love one another with a pure heart fervently:	—love one another from the heart fervently:
23	Being born again,	—having been begotten again,
	—for ever.	*omitted.*
24	—glory of man	—glory thereof
	—the flower thereof falleth away:	—the flower falleth:
25	—endureth	—abideth
	—the word which by the gospel is preached	—the word of good tidings which was preached
2 1	Wherefore laying aside all malice,	Putting away therefore all wickedness,

Chap.	Authorized Version.	Revised Version.
2	—desire the sincere milk of the word, that ye may grow thereby:	—long for the spiritual milk which is without guile, that ye may grow thereby unto salvation;
3	If so be ye have	—if ye have
4	To whom coming as unto a living stone, disallowed indeed of men, but chosen of God, and precious,	—unto whom coming, a living stone, rejected indeed of men, but with God elect, precious,
5	—lively	—living
	—an holy priesthood,	—to be a holy priesthood,
6	Wherefore also	Because
	—confounded.	—put to shame.
7	Unto you therefore which believe he is precious: but unto them which be disobedient,	For you therefore which believe is the preciousness: but for such as disbelieve,
	—disallowed,	—rejected,
8	—even to them which stumble	—for they stumble
9	—a chosen generation,	—an elect race,
	—a peculiar people;	—a people for God's own possession,
	—praises	—excellencies
11	Dearly beloved,	Beloved,
12	—your conversation honest	—your behaviour seemly
	—whereas	—wherein
13	Submit yourselves	Be subject
14	—as unto them that are	—as sent by him for

Chap.	Authorized Version.	Revised Version.
	sent by him for the punishment of evil-doers,	vengeance on evil-doers
16	—liberty	—freedom
	—maliciousness,	—wickedness,
	—the servants	—bondservants
18	—be subject	—be in subjection
19	—thankworthy,	—acceptable,
20	—when ye be buffeted for your faults,	—when ye sin, and are buffeted for it,
21	—leaving us	—leaving you
24	—being dead	—having died
25	—as sheep going astray;	—going astray like sheep;
3 1	Likewise,	In like manner,
	—if any	—even if any
	—be won by the conversation	—be gained by the behaviour
2	While they behold your chaste conversation	—beholding your chaste behaviour
3	—wearing of gold,	—wearing jewels of gold,
4	—in that which is not corruptible, even the ornament	—in the incorruptible apparel
5	—in the old time	—aforetime
	—trusted	—hoped
6	—whose daughters ye are, as long as ye do well, and are not afraid with any amazement.	—whose children ye are now, if ye do well, and are not put in fear by any terror.
7	—with them	—with your wives

Chap.	Authorized Version.	Revised Version.
7	—the wife,	—the woman,
	—heirs together	—joint-heirs
8	Finally, be ye all of one mind, having compassion one of another, love as brethren, be pitiful, be courteous:	Finally, be ye all likeminded, compassionate, loving as brethren, tenderhearted, humbleminded:
9	—railing for railing:	—reviling for reviling;
	—knowing that ye are thereunto called,	—for hereunto were ye called,
11	—eschew	—turn away from
	—ensue	—pursue
12	—over	—upon
	—are open unto their prayers:	—unto their supplication:
	—against	—upon
13	—followers	—zealous
14	—happy	—blessed
	—be not afraid of their terror,	—fear not their fear,
15	But sanctify the Lord God in your hearts:	—but sanctify in your hearts Christ as Lord:
	—of the hope	—concerning the hope
16	—that, whereas they speak evil of you, as of evil doers, they may be ashamed that falsely accuse your good conversation in Christ.	—that, wherein ye are spoken against, they may be put to shame who revile your good manner of life in Christ.
17	—be so,	—should so will,
18	For Christ also hath	Because Christ also

Chap.	Authorized Version.	Revised Version.
	once suffered for sins, the just for the unjust,	suffered for sins once, the righteous for the unrighteous,
18	—by the Spirit:	—in the spirit;
19	By which	—in which
20	—sometime	—aforetime
	—when once	—when
	—by water.	—through water:
21	The like figure whereunto even baptism doth also now save us	—which also after a true likeness doth now save you, even baptism,
	—the answer	—the interrogation
22	Who is gone into heaven, and is on the right hand of God;	—who is on the right hand of God, having gone into heaven;
4 3	—of our life	*omitted.*
	—the will	—the desire
	—when we walked	—and to have walked
	—excess of wine,	—wine-bibbings,
	—banquetings,	—carousings,
6	—for this cause	—unto this end
	—also to them that are dead,	—even to the dead,
7	—sober, and watch unto prayer.	—of sound mind, and be sober unto prayer:
8	—have fervent charity	—being fervent in your love
	—for charity shall cover	—for love covereth
9	—grudging.	—murmuring:
10	As every man hath received the gift, even	—according as each hath received a gift, min-

Chap.	Authorized Version.	Revised Version.
	so minister the same one to another,	istering it among yourselves,
11	If any man speak, let him speak as the oracles of God; if any man minister, let him do it as of the ability which God giveth:	—if any man speaketh, speaking as it were oracles of God; if any man ministereth, ministering as of the strength which God supplieth:
	—to whom be praise and dominion	—whose is the glory and the dominion
12	—the fiery trial which is to try you,	—the fiery trial among you, which cometh upon you to prove you,
13	—when his glory shall be revealed,	—at the revelation of his glory
	—be glad	—rejoice
14	—happy	—blessed
	—for the spirit of glory and of God	—because the Spirit of glory and the Spirit of God
15	—busybody	—meddler
16	—on this behalf.	—in this name.
19	—commit the keeping of their souls to him in well doing, as unto a faithful Creator.	—commit their souls in well-doing unto a faithful Creator.
5 1	—which are among you	—therefore among you
	—also an elder,	—a fellow-elder,
2	Feed	Tend
	—taking the oversight thereof,	—exercising the oversight,

Chap.	Authorized Version.	Revised Version.
2	—willingly;	—willingly, according unto God;
3	Neither as being lords over God's heritage, but being ensamples	—neither as lording it over the charge allotted to you, but making yourselves ensamples
4	—shall appear,	—shall be manifested,
5	—submit yourselves	—be subject
	—be subject one to another, and be clothed with humility:	—gird yourselves with humility, to serve one another:
7	—care	—anxiety
8	—be vigilant;	—be watchful:
9	—resist	—withstand
	—afflictions	—sufferings
10	—by Christ Jesus,	—in Christ,
	—a while, make you perfect,	—a little while, shall himself perfect,
11	—be glory and dominion	—be the dominion
12	—a faithful brother unto you, as I suppose,	—our faithful brother, as I account him,
	—wherein ye stand.	—stand ye fast therein.
13	The church that is at Babylon,	She that is in Babylon,
	—Marcus	—Mark
14	Greet ye	Salute
	—charity.	—love.
	—with you	—unto you
	—Christ Jesus.	—Christ.
	—Amen.	*omitted.*

II. PETER.

Chap.	Authorized Version.	Revised Version.
1 1	—through the righteousness	—in the righteousness
2	Grace and peace be multiplied unto you	Grace to you and peace be multiplied
3	According as	—seeing that
	—to glory and virtue:	—by his own glory and virtue;
4	Whereby are given unto us exceeding great and precious promises:	—whereby he hath granted unto us his precious and exceeding great promises;
	—that by these ye might be	—that through these ye may become
5	And beside this, giving all diligence, add to your faith virtue; and to virtue knowledge;	Yea, and for this very cause adding on your part all diligence, in your faith supply virtue; and in your virtue knowledge;
6	And to	—and in your
	(*Also similar expressions in vv. 6 and 7*).	
7	—brotherly kindness;	—love of the brethren;
	—charity.	—love.
8	—be in you,	—are yours
	—that ye shall neither be barren nor unfruitful	—to be not idle nor unfruitful

Chap.	Authorized Version.	Revised Version.
9	—and cannot see afar off, and hath forgotten that he was purged	—seeing only what is near, having forgotten the cleansing
10	Wherefore the rather, brethren, give diligence	Wherefore, brethren, give the more diligence
	—fall :	—stumble :
11	For so an entrance shall be ministered unto you abundantly	—for thus shall be richly supplied unto you the entrance
12	—I will not be negligent	—I shall be ready always
	—in the present truth.	—in the truth which is with you.
13	Yea, I think it meet,	And I think it right,
14	—shortly I must put off this tabernacle,	—the putting off of my tabernacle cometh swiftly,
	—hath shewed me.	—signified unto me.
15	Moreover I will endeavour that ye may be able after my decease to have these things always in remembrance.	Yea, I will give diligence that at every time ye may be able after my decease to call these things to remembrance.
18	—which came from heaven we heard,	—we ourselves heard came out of heaven,
19	We have also a more sure word of prophecy ;	And we have the word of prophecy made more sure ;
	—a light that shineth	—a lamp shining
21	For the prophecy came not in old time	For no prophecy ever came
	—but holy men of God spake as they were moved	—but men spake from God, being moved

Chap.	Authorized Version.	Revised Version.
2 1	—there were	—there arose
	—damnable heresies, even denying the Lord	—destructive heresies, denying even the Master
2	—pernicious ways;	—lascivious doings;
3	—whose judgment now of a long time	—whose sentence now from of old
	—damnation	—destruction
4	—that sinned,	—when they sinned,
	—delivered them into chains	—committed them to pits
5	—old	—ancient
	—Noah the eighth person,	—Noah with seven others,
	—bringing in the flood	—when he brought a flood
6	—ensample	—example
7	—just Lot, vexed with the filthy conversation of the wicked:	—righteous Lot, sore distressed by the lascivious life of the wicked
8	—unlawful	—lawless
9	—and to reserve the unjust unto the day of judgment to be punished:	—and to keep the unrighteous under punishment unto the day of judgement.
10	—uncleanness,	—defilement,
	—government. Presumptuous are they,	—dominion. Daring,
	—they are not afraid to speak evil of dignities,	—they tremble not to rail at dignities:
11	—which are	—though
	—accusation	—judgement

Chap.	Authorized Version.	Revised Version.
12	—as natural brute beasts, made to be taken and destroyed, speak evil of the things that they understand not; and shall utterly perish in their own corruption;	—as creatures without reason, born mere animals to be taken and destroyed, railing in matters whereof they are ignorant, shall in their destroying surely be destroyed, suffering wrong as the hire of wrong doing; men that count it pleasure to revel
13	And shall receive the reward of unrighteousness, as they that count it pleasure to riot	
	—sporting themselves with their own deceivings	—revelling in their love-feasts
14	—beguiling unstable souls:	—enticing unstedfast souls;
	—covetous practices; cursed children:	—covetousness; children of cursing;
15	Which have forsaken	—forsaking
	—and are gone	—they went
	—Bosor,	—Beor,
	—wages of unrighteousness;	—hire of wrong-doing;
16	—his iniquity:	—his own transgression:
	—forbad	—stayed
17	—wells	—springs
	—clouds that are carried with a tempest; to whom the mist of darkness is reserved for ever.	—mists driven by a storm; for whom the blackness of darkness hath been reserved.
18	For when they speak	For, uttering
	—allure through the	—entice in the lusts of

Chap.		Authorized Version.	Revised Version.
		lusts of the flesh, through much wantonness, those that were clean escaped	the flesh, by lasciviousness, those who are just escaping
	19	—the servants	—bondservants
	20	—pollutions	—defilements
		—the latter end is worse with them than the beginning.	—the last state is become worse with them than the first.
	22	But it is happened	It has happened
3	1	—pure minds by way of remembrance:	—sincere mind by putting you in remembrance;
	2	—may be mindful	—should remember
		—and the commandment of us the apostles of the Lord and Saviour:	—and the commandment of the Lord and Saviour through your apostles:
	3	—there shall come in the last days scoffers,	—in the last days mockers shall come with mockery,
	4	—for since	—for, from the day that
	5	—willingly are ignorant of,	—wilfully forget,
		—that by the word of God the heavens were of old, and the earth standing out of the water and in the water:	—that there were heavens from of old, and an earth compacted out of water and amidst water, by the word of God;
	6	Whereby	—by which means
	7	—are kept in store, and reserved unto fire against the day of	—have been stored up for fire, being reserved against the

Chap.	Authorized Version.	Revised Version.
	judgment and perdition	day of judgement and destruction
8	But, beloved, be not ignorant of this one thing,	But forget not this one thing, beloved,
9	—us-ward,	—you-ward,
	—willing	—wishing
10	—shall melt	—shall be dissolved
11	—conversation	—living
12	—hasting unto	—earnestly desiring
	—wherein	—by reason of which
13	Nevertheless	But,
14	—be diligent	—give diligence
	—found of him	—found
	—blameless.	—blameless in his sight.
16	—in which	—wherein
	—they that are unlearned and unstable	—the ignorant and unstedfast
17	—seeing ye know these things before,	—knowing these things beforehand
	—led away	—carried away

Purvey.   W.
Tyndale 1534.   T.
Great 1539   Gr.
Geneva 1557   G
Rheims 1582.   R.

I. JOHN.

2. 16   I. JOHN.   303

Chap.		Authorized Version.	Revised Version.
1	1	—have looked upon, T. Gr.	—beheld, W.
		—of the Word W. T. Gr. G. R	—concerning the Word
	2	—shew unto you that eternal life, T. Gr. G	—declare unto you the life [the] eternal [life,] R.
	3	—and truly our fellowship	—yea, and our fellowship
	4	—write we unto you, W. T. G. G. R that your joy may be full. W. T. G. G. R.	—we write, that our joy may be fulfilled.
	5	—declare T. Gr. G. R.	—announce
	7	—Jesus Christ W. T. Gr. G. R.	—Jesus
	9	—just W. T. Gr. G. R.	—righteous
2	1	—advocate W. T. Gr.	—Advocate 1611 ed. A.V. G.
	2	—but also for the sins of W. T. Gr. G.	—but also for [G.]:
	7	Brethren, I write no new commandment unto you, (W). T. Gr. G. (R)	Beloved, no new commandment write I unto you,
		—from the beginning. (End of verse). T. Gr. G.	omitted. W. R.
	8	—is past, W. T. Gr. G. R.	—is passing away,
		—now shineth. W. T. Gr. G. R	—already shineth.
	13	—wicked one. (W/(T) Gr) R (Also in v. 14). A G.	—evil one. G.
	16	—pride of life, W. (T) G. G. R.	—vainglory of life,

Chap.	Authorized Version.	Revised Version.
18	—last time : T. Gr. G.	—last hour : W. R.
	—shall come, T. Gr. G.	—cometh, W. R.
19	—they would no doubt T.	—they would (W.)
20	—unction R.	—anointing W. (T.) Gr. G.
21	—and that (T.)(Gr.) G. R.	—because (W)
22	—He is antichrist, that denieth (T.)(Gr.)(G.)(R.)	This is the antichrist, (W) even he that denieth
23	—[but] he that acknowledgeth W. Gr.	—he that confesseth R.
24	Let that therefore abide in you, T. Gr. G.	As for you, let that abide in you (R)
	—shall remain T. Gr. G.	—abide W. R.
	—continue T. Gr. G.	—abide R.
25	—eternal life.	—the life eternal.
26	—that seduce you. R.	—that would lead you astray.
27	But G.	And as for you W. T. Gr. R.
	—the same anointing teacheth you in all things, of Gr. G. R.	—his anointing teacheth you concerning all things,
	—truth	—true W. T. Gr. G. R.
	—ye shall abide (G.)	—ye abide
28	—when he shall appear, W. T. Gr. G. R.	—if he shall be manifested,
	—confidence, R.	—boldness, (T. Gr. G.)
29	—born W. T. Gr. G. R.	—begotten
3 1	—the sons of God :	—children of God: and such we are. (W)(Gr) (R)
2	—the sons W. T. Gr. G. R.	—children
	—it doth not yet appear (W)(T.)(Gr)(G)(R)	—it is not yet made manifest
	—when he shall appear, W. T. Gr. G. R.	—if he shall be manifested,

I. JOHN.

Chap.	Authorized Version.	Revised Version.
3	—every man W.T.G.G.	—every one R
	—in him W.T.Gn G. R	—set on him
4	Whosoever (committeth sin) transgresseth also the law: for sin is the transgression of the law.	(Every one that) doeth sin doeth also lawlessness: and sin is lawlessness.
7	—deceive you: W.T.G.G.	—lead you astray:
8	—committeth T.G.G.R.	—doeth W.
	—For this purpose T.G.G	—To this end
9	—born of God doth not commit sin; R.	—begotten of God doeth W. no sin,
	—remaineth T.G.G.	—abideth R.
12	—that wicked one,	—the evil one,
14	—his brother T.G.G.	omitted. W.R.
16	Hereby perceive we the love of God W.R.	Hereby know we love,
17	—this world's W.T.Gn G.	—the world's R.
	—seeth W.G.G.	—beholdeth
	—bowels of compassion	—compassion T.G.G.
	—how dwelleth the love of God W.T.Gn G.	—how doth the love of God abide R
20	For if Gn G.R	—whereinsoever (W)
21	—then have we confidence R	—we have boldness
24	—dwelleth W.T.G.G.	—abideth R.
4 1	—try	—prove W.T.Gn G.R
3	—that Jesus Christ is come in the flesh	—Jesus W.R
	—that it should come; and even now already is it in the world.	—that it cometh; and now it is in the world already.

I. JOHN.

Chap.	Authorized Version.	Revised Version.
5	—of the world, W. T. G. G. R	—as of the world,
6	—Hereby know we T. G. G.	—By this we know (W) (R)
7	—born W. T. G. G. R.	—begotten
9	W. T. G. G. R. —In this was manifested the love of God toward us, T. G. G.	Herein was the love of God manifested in us, W. R
12	—seen W. T. G. G. R.	—beheld
	—dwelleth W. T. G. G.	—abideth R.
13	—dwell W. T. G. G.	—abide R.
14	—we have seen and do testify T. G. G R.	—we have beheld and bear witness (W)
16	—dwelleth W. T. G. G. —dwelleth W. T. G. G. —and God in him. W. T. G. G. R.	—abideth R —abideth R —and God abideth in him.
17	Herein is our love made perfect,	Herein is love made (G)(R) perfect with us, (W)(T)(G)
18	—torment.	—punishment ;
19	We love him, (W) T. G. G.	We love,
20	—how can he love God (W) (T) (Gr) G. (R)	—cannot love God
5 1	—born W. T. G. G. R	—begotten
2	—keep T. G. G. R.	—do (W)
4	—born W T. Gr. G. R.	—begotten
7	For there are three W that bear record in Gr. heaven, the Father, the Word, and the (R) Holy Ghost : and these three are one.	} omitted.
8	W. Gr. G. R And there are three W. that bear witness in earth. W. G. R.	For there are three who bear witness, T. Gr.
9	—testified of T. Gr. G. R aorist.	—borne witness concerning

5. 21   I. JOHN.   307

Chap.	Authorized Version.	Revised Version.
10	—the record that God gave of his Son.	—the witness that God hath borne concerning his Son.
11	And this is the record,	And the witness is this,
13	—that believe on the name of the Son of God;	} omitted. W. R.
14	—the confidence which we have in him,	—the boldness which we have toward him,
15	—desired	—asked
16	—he shall give	—God will give
	—I do not say that he shall pray for it.	—not concerning this do I say that he should make request.
18	—born	—begotten
	—wicked one	—evil one
19	—wickedness.	—the evil one.
21	—keep	—guard
	—Amen.	omitted.

II. JOHN.

II. JOHN.

P.	Authorized Version.	Revised Version.
3	Grace be with you, mercy, and peace,	Grace, mercy, peace shall be with us,
	—the Lord Jesus Christ,	—Jesus Christ,
4	—of thy children	—certain of thy children
7	—entered	—gone forth
	—who confess not	—even they that confess not
	—is come	—cometh
9	—transgresseth,	—goeth onward
	—doctrine (*Also in v.* 10).	—teaching
10	—neither bid him God speed :	—and give him no greeting :
11	—he that biddeth him God speed is partaker of his evil deeds.	—he that giveth him greeting partaketh in his evil works.
12	—trust	—hope
	—our joy may be full.	—your joy may be fulfilled.
13	—greet	—salute
	—Amen.	*omitted.*

III. JOHN.

Chap.	Authorized Version.	Revised Version.
1	—the wellbeloved Gaius,	—Gaius the beloved,
2	—I wish above all things	—I pray that in all things
3	—testified of the truth that is in thee,	—bear witness unto thy truth,
4	I have no greater joy	Greater joy have I none
5	—thou doest faithfully whatsoever thou doest to the brethren, and to strangers;	—thou doest a faithful work in whatsoever thou doest toward them that are brethren and strangers withal;
6	—of thy charity	—to thy love
	—whom if thou bring forward on their journey after a godly sort, thou shalt do well:	—whom thou wilt do well to set forward on their journey worthily of God:
7	—for his name's sake	—for the sake of the Name
8	—receive	—welcome
	—fellowhelpers to the truth.	—fellow-workers with the truth.
9	I wrote	I wrote somewhat
10	Wherefore,	Therefore,

Chap.	Authorized Version.	Revised Version.
10	—remember his deeds	—bring to remembrance his works
	—malicious	—wicked
11	—follow	—imitate
12	—good report	—the witness
	—record;	—witness;
13	—to write,	—to write unto thee,
	—I will not with ink and pen write unto thee:	—I am unwilling to write them to thee with ink and pen:
14	—trust	—hope
	Our friends	The friends
	—Greet	—Salute

JUDE.

Chap.	Authorized Version.	Revised Version.
1	—to them that are sanctified by God the Father, and preserved in Jesus Christ, and called:	—to them that are called, beloved in God the Father, and kept by Jesus Christ:
3	—when I gave	—while I was giving
	—it was needful for me to write unto you, and exhort you that ye should earnestly contend	—I was constrained to write unto you exhorting you to contend earnestly
4	—unawares, who were before of old ordained	—privily, even they who were of old set forth
	—denying the only Lord God, and our Lord Jesus Christ.	—denying our only Master and Lord, Jesus Christ.
5	I will therefore put	Now I desire to put
	—though ye once knew this,	—though ye know all things once for all,
6	—first estate,	—own principality,
	—own habitation, he hath reserved in everlasting chains	—proper habitation, he hath kept in everlasting bonds
7	—in like manner, giving themselves over	—in like manner with these given themselves over

Chap.	Authorized Version.	Revised Version.
7	—vengeance	—punishment
8	Likewise also these filthy dreamers defile the flesh, despise dominion, and speak evil of dignities.	Yet in like manner these also in their dreamings defile the flesh, and set at nought dominion, and rail at dignities.
9	—accusation,	—judgement,
10	—speak evil of those things	—rail at whatsoever things
	—know	—understand
	—as brute beasts, in those things they corrupt themselves.	—like the creatures without reason, in these things are they destroyed.
11	—ran greedily after the error of Balaam for reward,	—ran riotously in the error of Balaam for hire,
	—Core.	—Korah.
12	These are spots in your feasts of charity, when they feast with you, feeding themselves without fear: clouds are they without water, carried about of winds; trees whose fruit withereth, without fruit,	These are they who are hidden rocks in your love-feasts when they feast with you, shepherds that without fear feed themselves; clouds without water, carried along by winds; autumn trees without fruit,
13	Raging	—wild
14	And Enoch also, the seventh from Adam, prophesied of these,	And to these also Enoch, the seventh from Adam, prophesied,
	—saints,	—holy ones,

Chap.	Authorized Version.	Revised Version.
15	—convince	—convict
	—ungodly deeds	—works of ungodliness
	—committed,	—wrought,
	—their hard speeches	—the hard things
16	—having men's persons in admiration because of advantage.	—shewing respect of persons for the sake of advantage.
17	—of the apostles	—by the apostles
18	—they told you	—they said to you,
19	—who separate themselves,	—who make separations,
20	—Ghost,	—Spirit,
22	And of some have compassion, making a difference:	And on some have mercy, who are in doubt;
23	And others save with fear, pulling them out of the fire;	—and some save, snatching them out of the fire; and on some have mercy with fear;
24	—to keep you from falling, and to present you faultless before the presence of his glory with exceeding joy,	—to guard you from stumbling, and to set you before the presence of his glory without blemish in exceeding joy,
25	—only wise God our Saviour,	—only God our Saviour, through Jesus Christ our Lord,
	—both now and ever.	—before all time, and now, and for evermore.

REVELATION.

Chap.		Authorized Version.	Revised Version.
1	1	—things	—even the things
	2	—record	—witness
		—and of all things	—even of all things
	5	—first begotten	—firstborn
		—prince	—ruler
		—washed us from our sins in his own blood,	—loosed us from our sins by his blood;
	6	And hath made us kings and priests unto God and his Father;	—and he made us to be a kingdom, to be priests unto his God and Father;
	7	—all kindreds of the earth shall wail because of him.	—all the tribes of the earth shall mourn over him.
	8	—the beginning and the ending,	} *omitted.*
	9	—who also am your brother, and companion in tribulation,	—your brother and partaker with you in the tribulation
		—of Jesus Christ,	—which are in Jesus,
		—Jesus Christ.	—Jesus.
	11	—I am Alpha and Omega, the first and the last: and,	} *omitted.*
		—which are in Asia;	*omitted.*
		—Pergamos,	—Pergamum,

Chap.	Authorized Version.	Revised Version.
12	—being turned,	—having turned
13	—the Son of man,	—a son of man,
	—paps	—breasts
14	—like wool,	—as white wool,
15	—fine brass, as if they burned in a furnace;	—burnished brass, as if it had been refined in a furnace;
	—sound	—voice
16	—went	—proceeded
17	—as dead.	—as one dead.
	—the last:	—the Living one;
18	I am he that liveth and was dead;	—and I was dead,
	—of hell and of death.	—of death and of Hades.
19	Write the things which thou hast seen,	Write therefore the things which thou sawest,
2 2	—labour,	—toil
	—them which are evil:	—evil men,
	—which say they are	—which call themselves
	—hast found them liars:	—didst find them false;
3	And hast borne, and hast patience, and for my name's sake hast laboured, and hast not fainted.	—and thou hast patience and didst bear for my name's sake, and hast not grown weary.
4	Nevertheless I have somewhat against thee, because thou hast left	But I have this against thee, that thou didst leave
5	—I will come unto thee quickly,	—I come to thee,

Chap.	Authorized Version.	Revised Version.
7	—which is in the midst of the paradise of God.	—which is in the Paradise of God.
8	—is alive;	—lived again;
9	—works, and	*omitted.*
10	—thou shalt suffer:	—thou art about to suffer:
	—shall cast	—is about to cast
12	—Permagos	—Pergamum
	—the sharp sword with two edges;	—the sharp two-edged sword:
13	—thy works, and	*omitted.*
	—seat	—throne
	—wherein Antipas was my faithful martyr,	—of Antipas my witness, my faithful one,
	—slain	—killed
14	—doctrine (*Also in v.* 15).	—teaching
15	—which thing I hate.	—in like manner.
16	Repent;	Repent therefore;
	—fight	—make war
17	—I give to eat	—I give
	—in the stone	—upon the stone
18	—like fine brass;	—like unto burnished brass:
19	I know thy works, and charity, and service, and faith, and thy patience, and thy works; and the last to be more than the first.	I know thy works, and thy love and faith and ministry and patience, and that thy last works are more than the first.
20	Notwithstanding I have a few things against thee,	But I have this against thee,

Chap.	Authorized Version.	Revised Version.
21	And I gave her space to repent of her fornication; and she repented not.	And I gave her time that she should repent; and she willeth not to repent of her fornication.
22	—of their deeds.	—of her works.
24	—doctrine,	—teaching,
	—depths of Satan, as they speak; I will put upon you	—deep things of Satan, as they say; I cast upon you
25	But that which ye have already	Howbeit that which ye have,
26	—power	—authority
27	—shall they be broken	—are broken
3 2	—strengthen	—stablish
	—I have not found thy works perfect before God.	—I have found no works of thine fulfilled before my God.
3	—hold fast,	—keep it,
5	—the same shall be clothed in white raiment;	—shall thus be arrayed in white garments;
	—I will not	—I will in no wise
8	—an open door, and no man can shut it:	—a door opened, which none can shut),
	—strength,	—power,
9	Behold, I will make them of the synagogue of Satan,	Behold, I give of the synagogue of Satan,
10	—temptation,	—trial,
11	Behold, I come	I come
12	—go no more out:	—go out thence no more:
	—and I will write upon him my new name.	—and mine own new name.

Chap.		Authorized Version.	Revised Version.
	14	—of the Laodiceans	—in Laodicea
	16	—neither cold nor hot,	—neither hot nor cold,
	17	—and increased with goods,	—and have gotten riches,
		—wretched,	—the wretched one
	18	—tried in the fire,	—refined by fire,
		—raiment,	—garments,
		—be clothed,	—clothe thyself,
		—do not appear;	—be not made manifest;
	19	—rebuke	—reprove
	21	To him that overcometh will I grant	He that overcometh, I will give to him
		—am set	—sat
4	1	After this I looked,	After these things I saw,
		—talking with me; which said,	—speaking with me, one saying,
		—must be	—must come to pass
	2	And immediately	Straightway
	3	—a jasper and a sardine stone:	—a jasper stone and a sardius:
		—in sight like unto an emerald.	—like an emerald to look upon.
	4	—seats:	—thrones:
		—clothed in white raiment;	—arrayed in white garments;
	5	—thunderings and voices:	—voices and thunders.
	6	—there was a sea of glass	—as it were a glassy sea
		—were four beasts	—four living creatures
	7	—beast	—creature
	8	—beasts	—living creatures,

Chap.	Authorized Version.	Revised Version.
8	—had each of them six wings about him; and they were full of eyes within:	—having each one of them six wings, are full of eyes round about and within:
	—Lord God Almighty,	—is the Lord God, the Almighty,
9	—when those beasts give glory	—when the living creatures shall give glory
11	—O Lord,	—our Lord and our God,
	—for thy pleasure they are	—because of thy will they were,
5 1	—on the backside, sealed	—on the back, close sealed
2	—loud voice,	—great voice,
3	—no man	—no one
4	—to open and to read the book, neither to look thereon.	—to open the book, or to look thereon:
5	—prevailed	—overcome,
	—and to loose the seven	—and the seven
6	And I beheld, and, lo,	And I saw
	—beasts	—living creatures
7	—and took the book	—and he taketh it
8	—beasts	—living creatures
	—every one of them harps, and golden vials full of odours,	—each one a harp, and golden bowls full of incense,
9	—and hast redeemed us to God by thy blood out of every kindred,	—and didst purchase unto God with thy blood men of every tribe,
10	—hast made us	—madest them to be
	—kings	—a kingdom

Chap.	Authorized Version.	Revised Version.
10	—we shall reign	—they reign
11	—beheld,	—saw,
	—beasts	—living creatures
12	—loud	—great
	—strength,	—might,
13	—creature	—created thing
	—such as are in the sea,	—on the sea,
	—Blessing, and honour, and glory, and power, be unto him that sitteth upon the throne, and unto the Lamb for ever and ever.	—Unto him that sitteth on the throne, and unto the Lamb, be the blessing, and the honour, and the glory, and the dominion, for ever and ever.
14	—beasts	—living creatures
	—the four and twenty elders	—the elders
	—that liveth for ever and ever.	} *omitted.*
6 1	—the seals,	—the seven seals,
	—as it were the noise of thunder, one of the four beasts saying, Come and see.	—one of the four living creatures saying as with a voice of thunder, Come.
2	—went forth	—came forth
3	—the second beast say, Come and see.	—the second living creature saying, Come.
4	And there went out another horse that was red:	And another horse came forth, a red horse:
	—power was given	—it was given

Chap.	Authorized Version.	Revised Version.
4	—kill	—slay
5	—the third beast say, Come and see.	—the third living creature saying, Come.
	—beheld,	—saw,
	—on him	—thereon
	—a pair of balances	—a balance
6	—heard	—heard as it were
	—beasts say,	—living creatures saying,
	—and see thou hurt not the oil and the wine.	—and the oil and the wine hurt thou not.
7	—beast say, Come and see.	—living creature saying, Come.
8	—Hell	—Hades
	—power	—authority
	—hunger,	—famine,
	—with the beasts	—by the wild beasts
9	—under	—underneath
10	—O Lord, holy and true,	—O Master, the holy and true,
11	And white robes were given unto every one of them;	And there was given them to each one a white robe;
12	—beheld	—saw
	—the moon	—the whole moon
13	—untimely	—unripe
	—great	—mighty
14	—departed as a scroll when it is rolled together;	—was removed as a scroll when it is rolled up;
15	—the great men, and the rich men, and the chief captains, and the mighty men,	—the princes, and the chief captains, and the rich, and the strong,

21

Chap.	Authorized Version.	Revised Version.
15	—dens	—caves
17	—his wrath	—their wrath
7 1	And after these things	After this
2	—the east,	—the sunrising,
4	—and there were sealed	*omitted.*
9	After this I beheld, and, lo,	After these things I saw, and behold,
	—of all nations, and kindreds, and people,	—out of every nation, and of all tribes and peoples
	—clothed with	—arrayed in
11	—beasts,	—living creatures;
13	—What are these which are arrayed in white robes?	—These which are arrayed in the white robes, who are they,
14	—Sir,	—My Lord,
15	—shall dwell among them.	—shall spread his tabernacle over them.
16	—light on them,	—strike upon them,
17	—shall feed them, and shall lead them unto living fountains of waters:	—shall be their shepherd, and shall guide them unto fountains of waters of life;
8 1	—there was silence	—there followed a silence
3	—at the altar,	—over the altar,
	—offer it with the prayers	—add it unto the prayers
4	—ascended	—went
5	—into	—upon
	—voices, and thunderings,	—thunders, and voices,
7	*inserted.*	—and the third part of the earth was burnt up,

Chap.		Authorized Version.	Revised Version.
	10	—as it were a lamp,	—as a torch,
	12	—the day shone not	—the day should not shine
		—likewise.	—in like manner.
	13	—beheld,	—saw,
		—through the midst of heaven,	—in mid heaven,
		—to the inhabiters of the earth	—for them that dwell on the earth,
9	1	—bottomless pit. (*Also in v.* 2).	—pit of the abyss.
	3	—unto them was given power,	—power was given them,
	4	—commanded them	—said unto them
	6	—shall not	—shall in no wise
	7	—unto battle ;	—for war ;
		—the faces of men.	—men's faces.
	9	—running to battle.	—rushing to war.
	10	—and there were stings in their tails : and their power was to hurt	—and stings ; and in their tails is their power to hurt
	11	And they had a king over them, which is the angel of the bottomless pit,	They have over them as king the angel of the abyss :
	12	One woe	The first Woe
	13	—the four horns	—the horns
	14	—bound in	—bound at
	15	—for to slay	—that they should kill
	16	—were two hundred thousand thousand :	—was twice ten thousand times ten thousand :
	17	—jacinth,	—hyacinth

Chap.		Authorized Version.	Revised Version.
	17	—issued	—proceedeth
	18	—these three	—these three plagues
		—issued	—proceeded
	19	—their power	—the power of the horses
	20	—the men	—mankind,
10	1	—mighty	—strong
		—clothed	—arrayed
	3	—loud	—great
	5	—his hand	—his right hand
	7	—when he shall begin	—when he is about
		—the mystery of God should be finished, as he hath declared	—then is finished the mystery of God, according to the good tidings which he declared
	8	—spake unto me again,	—I heard it again speaking with me,
		—the little book	—the book
	10	—as soon as	—when
	11	—he said	—they say
		—before	—over
11	1	—and the angel stood, saying,	—and one said,
	2	—leave out,	—leave without,
		—it is given unto the Gentiles:	—it hath been given unto the nations:
	3	—give power	—give
	4	—God	—Lord
	5	—will hurt them, (1)	—desireth to hurt them,
		—will hurt them, (2)	—shall desire to hurt them,

Chap.	Authorized Version.	Revised Version.
6	—all plagues, —they will.	—every plague, —they shall desire.
7	—ascendeth out of the bottomless pit	—cometh up out of the abyss
8	—our Lord	—their Lord
9	And they of the people and kindreds —shall see —put in graves.	And from among the peoples and tribes —do men look upon —laid in a tomb.
11	—the Spirit —saw	—the breath —beheld
12	—ascended up to	—went up into
13	—the same hour —and in the earthquake were slain of men seven thousand :	—in that hour —and there were killed in the earthquake seven thousand persons :
14	—woe	—Woe
15	—there were —The kingdoms of this world are	—there followed —The kingdom of the world is
16	—seats,	—thrones,
17	—God Almighty, —and art to come;	—God, the Almighty, *omitted.*
18	—angry, —that they should be judged, and that thou shouldest give reward unto	—wroth, —to be judged, and the time to give their reward to
19	—testament : —thunderings,	—covenant; —thunders,
12 1	And there appeared a great wonder in heaven;	And a great sign was seen in heaven;

Chap.	Authorized Version.	Revised Version.
1	—clothed	—arrayed
3	—there appeared another wonder	—there was seen another sign
	—seven crowns upon his heads.	—upon his heads seven diadems.
4	—for to devour her child as soon as it was born.	—that when she was delivered, he might devour her child.
5	And she brought forth a man child,	And she was delivered of a son, a man child,
6	—that they should feed her there	—that there they may nourish her
7	—fought against the dragon;	—going forth to war with the dragon;
	—fought	—warred
9	—cast out,	—cast down,
	—which deceiveth	—the deceiver of
10	—loud voice saying in heaven,	—great voice in heaven,
	—strength,	—the power,
	—power	—authority
11	—by the blood	—because of the blood
	—by the word	—because of the word
	—their lives unto the death.	—their life even unto death.
12	—Woe to the inhabiters of the earth and of the sea!	Woe for the earth and for the sea:
	—because he knoweth	—knowing
15	—flood (*Also in v.* 16).	—river,
	—of the flood.	—by the stream.
17	—was wroth	—waxed wroth

Chap.	Authorized Version.	Revised Version.
17	—remnant	—rest
	—have the testimony of Jesus Christ.	—hold the testimony of Jesus:
13 1	—I stood	—he stood
	—saw	—I saw
	—rise up	—coming up
	—crowns,	—diadems,
	—the name	—names
2	—seat,	—throne,
3	—as it were wounded to death;	—as though it had been smitten unto death;
	—deadly wound	—death-stroke
4	—which gave power	—because he gave his authority
6	—in blasphemy	—for blasphemies
7	—and power was given him over all kindreds,	—and there was given to him authority over every tribe and people
8	—whose names are not written	—every one whose name hath not been written
	—slain	—that hath been slain
10	He that leadeth into captivity shall go into captivity: he that killeth with the sword must be killed with the sword.	If any man is for captivity, into captivity he goeth: if any man shall kill with the sword, with the sword must he be killed.
11	—beheld	—saw
12	—power	—authority
	—before him,	—in his sight.

Chap.	Authorized Version.	Revised Version.
12	—causeth	—maketh
	—deadly wound	—death-stroke
13	—wonders, so that he maketh fire come down from heaven	—signs, that he should even make fire to come down out of heaven
14	—by the means of those miracles which he had power to do	—by reason of the signs which it was given him to do
	—wound by a sword, and did live.	—stroke of the sword, and lived.
15	And he had power to give life unto the image of the beast,	And it was given unto him to give breath to it, even to the image of the beast,
16	—to receive a mark	—that there be given them a mark
17	—might buy or sell,	—should be able to buy or to sell,
	—or the name	—even the name
18	—threescore	—and sixty
14 1	—I looked, and, lo,	—I saw, and behold,
	—having his Father's name	—having his name, and the name of his Father,
2	—and I heard the voice of harpers	—and the voice which I heard was as the voice of harpers
3	—beasts,	—living creatures
	—which were redeemed from the earth.	—even they that had been purchased out of the earth.
4	—redeemed	—purchased
	—being the firstfruits	—to be the firstfruits

Chap.	Authorized Version.	Revised Version.
5	—no guile: for they are without fault before the throne of God.	—no lie: they are without blemish.
6	—in the midst of heaven, having the everlasting gospel to preach	—in mid heaven, having an eternal gospel to proclaim
	—kindred,	—tribe
7	Saying with a loud voice,	—and he saith with a great voice,
8	And there followed another angel, saying, Babylon is fallen, is fallen, that great city,	And another, a second angel, followed, saying, Fallen, fallen is Babylon the great,
9	—the third angel	—another angel, a third,
	—loud	—great
10	The same shall drink	—he also shall drink
	—which is poured out without mixture into the cup of his indignation;	—which is prepared unmixed in the cup of his anger;
11	—ascendeth	—goeth
12	—here are they that keep	—they that keep
13	—saying unto me,	—saying,
	—and their works do follow them.	—for their works follow with them.
14	—looked	—saw
	—one sat	—I saw one sitting
	—the Son of man,	—a son of man,
15	—loud	—great
	—Thrust in	—Send forth
	—the time is come for thee to reap;	—the hour to reap is come;

Chap.		Authorized Version.	Revised Version.
	15	—ripe.	—over-ripe.
	18	—cried with a loud cry	—called with a great voice
		—Thrust in	—Send forth
	19	—thrust in	—cast
		—vine	—vintage
	20	—by the space of	—as far as
15	1	—the seven last plagues;	—seven plagues, which are the last,
		—filled up	—finished
	2	—sea of glass	—glassy sea
		—had gotten the victory over	—come victorious from
		—over	—from
		—and over his mark,	*omitted.*
		—over the number	—from the number
		—stand on the sea of glass,	—standing by the glassy sea,
	3	—Lord God Almighty;	O Lord God, the Almighty;
		—just	—righteous
		—King of saints.	—King of the ages.
	4	—thy judgments are made	—thy righteous acts have been made
	5	—after that I looked, and, behold,	—after these things I saw,
	6	—clothed in pure and white linen, and having their breasts girded	—arrayed with precious stone, pure and bright, and girt about their breasts
	7	—beasts	—living creatures
		—vials	—bowls
	8	—were fulfilled.	—should be finished.

Chap.	Authorized Version.	Revised Version.
16 1	—Go your ways, and pour out the vials	—Go ye, and pour out the seven bowls
2	—vial (*And in subsequent verses*).	—bowl
3	—as the blood of a dead man: and every living soul died in the sea.	—blood as of a dead man; and every living soul died, even the things that were in the sea.
4	—upon the rivers and fountains of waters; and they became blood.	—into the rivers and the fountains of the waters; and it became blood.
5	—Thou art righteous, O Lord, which art and wast, and shalt be,	—Righteous art thou, which art and which wast, thou Holy One,
6	—shed	—poured out
7	And I heard another out of the altar say, Even so, Lord God Almighty,	And I heard the altar saying, Yea, O Lord God, the Almighty,
8	—power was given unto him	—it was given unto it
10	—seat	—throne
	—full of darkness;	—darkened;
11	—deeds.	—works.
12	—that the way of the kings of the east might be prepared.	—that the way might be made ready for the kings that come from the sunrising.
14	—miracles,	—signs;
	—of the earth and	*omitted*.
	—to gather them to the battle of that great	—to gather them together unto the war of

Chap.	Authorized Version.	Revised Version.
	day of God Almighty.	the great day of God, the Almighty.
16	—he gathered them	—they gathered them
	—in the Hebrew tongue Armageddon.	—in Hebrew Har-Magedon.
17	—the temple of heaven,	—the temple,
18	—so mighty an earthquake, and so great.	—so great an earthquake, so mighty.
19	—great Babylon came in remembrance before God,	—Babylon the great was remembered in the sight of God,
21	And there fell upon men a great hail out of heaven, every stone about the weight of a talent:	And great hail, every stone about the weight of a talent, cometh down out of heaven upon men.
17 1	—seven vials, and talked with me, saying unto me,	—seven bowls, and spake with me, saying,
2	—the inhabitants of the earth	—they that dwell in the earth
4	—scarlet colour,	—scarlet,
	—precious stones	—precious stone
	—and filthiness	—even the unclean things
6	—with great admiration.	—with a great wonder.
8	—and shall ascend out of the bottomless pit,	—and is about to come up out of the abyss,
	—whose names were not written	—they whose name hath not been written
	—that was, and is not, and yet is.	—how that he was, and is not, and shall come.

Chap.	Authorized Version.	Revised Version.
10	—there are	—they are
	—a short space.	—a little while.
11	—even he is the eighth,	—is himself also an eighth,
12	—but receive power as kings one hour with the beast.	—but they receive authority as kings, with the beast, for one hour.
13	—strength	—authority
14	—make war with	—war against
	—they that are with him are called,	—they also shall overcome that are with him, called
15	—whore (*Also in v.* 16).	—harlot
16	—upon the beast,	—and the beast,
	—and burn her	—and shall burn her utterly
17	—to fulfil his will, and to agree,	—to do his mind, and to come to one mind,
	—fulfilled.	—accomplished.
18 1	—power;	—authority;
2	—mightily with a strong voice,	—with a mighty voice,
	—Babylon the great is fallen, is fallen,	—Fallen, fallen is Babylon the great,
	—foul	—unclean
	—cage	—hold
3	For all nations have drunk of the wine of the wrath of her fornication,	For by the wine of the wrath of her fornication all the nations are fallen;

Chap.	Authorized Version.	Revised Version.
3	—through the abundance of her delicacies.	—by the power of her wantonness.
4	—Come out of her, my people, that ye be not partakers of	—Come forth, my people, out of her, that ye have no fellowship with
6	Render her even as she rewarded you,	Render unto her, even as she rendered,
	—which she hath filled, fill to her	—which she mingled, mingle unto her
7	—she hath	—soever she
	—lived deliciously,	—waxed wanton,
	—so much torment and sorrow give her:	—so much give her of torment and mourning:
	—shall see no sorrow.	—shall in no wise see mourning.
9	—deliciously	—wantonly
	—shall bewail her, and lament for her,	—shall weep and wail over her,
	—they shall see	—they look upon
10	—Alas, alas that great city Babylon, that mighty city!	—Woe, woe, the great city, Babylon, the strong city!
12	—all manner vessels	—every vessel
13	—and odours,	—and spice, and incense,
	—beasts,	—cattle,
	—and horses,	—and merchandise of horses
14	—departed	—gone
	—goodly are departed from thee, and thou	—sumptuous are perished from thee, and men

Chap.	Authorized Version.	Revised Version.
15	—wailing,	—mourning;
16	—Alas, alas that great city, that was clothed	—Woe, woe, the great city, she that was arrayed
17	—is come to nought.	—is made desolate.
	—and all the company in ships, and sailors, and as many as trade by sea,	—and every one that saileth any whither, and mariners, and as many as gain their living by sea,
18	—cried when they saw	—cried out as they looked upon
19	—wailing,	—mourning,
	—Alas, alas that great city,	—Woe, woe, the great city,
20	*inserted.*	—and ye saints,
	—avenged you	—judged your judgement
21	—mighty	—strong
	—like	—as it were
	—Thus with violence shall that great city Babylon be thrown down,	—Thus with a mighty fall shall Babylon, the great city, be cast down,
22	—musicians, and of pipers,	—minstrels and flute-players
	—sound	—voice
23	—candle	—lamp
	—great men	—princes
19 1	—much people	—a great multitude
	—and honour, and power, unto the Lord our God:	—and power, belong to our God:

Chap.	Authorized Version.	Revised Version.
2	—whore,	—harlot,
3	—again they said,	—a second time they say,
	—rose	—goeth
4	—beasts	—living creatures
5	—Praise our God,	—Give praise to our God,
6	—thunderings,	—thunders,
	—for the Lord God omnipotent reigneth.	—for the Lord our God, the Almighty, reigneth.
7	Let us be glad and rejoice, and give honour to him:	Let us rejoice and be exceeding glad, and let us give the glory unto him:
8	—to her was granted	—it was given unto her
	—be arrayed	—array herself
	—clean and white:	—bright and pure:
	—righteousness	—righteous acts
9	—called	—bidden
	—the true sayings	—true words
10	—fell at his feet	—fell down before his feet
	—thy fellowservant,	—a fellow-servant with thee
12	—were many crowns;	—are many diadems;
13	—he was clothed with a vesture dipped in blood:	—he is arrayed in a garment sprinkled with blood:
14	—clean.	—pure.
16	—vesture	—garment
17	—the fowls that fly in the midst of heaven, Come and gather	—the birds that fly in mid heaven, Come and be gathered to-

Chap.	Authorized Version.	Revised Version.
	yourselves together unto the supper of the great God;	gether unto the great supper of God;,
18	—mighty men,	—captains,
20	—miracles before him,	—the signs in his sight,
	—These both	—they twain
21	—the remnant were slain	—the rest were killed
	—which sword proceeded	—even the sword which came forth
	—fowls	—birds
20 1	—the bottomless pit (*Also in v.* **3**).	—the abyss
3	—and shut him up, and set a seal upon him,	—and shut it, and sealed it over him,
	—fulfilled:	—finished:
	—season.	—time.
4	—witness	—testimony
	—which had not worshipped the beast,	—such as worshipped not the beast,
5	—were finished.	—should be finished.
6	—on such	—over these
7	—expired,	—finished,
8	—go out	—come forth
	—quarters	—corners
	—to battle:	—to the war:
9	—from God	*omitted.*
12	—small and great, stand before God;	—the great and the small, standing before the throne;
13	—hell delivered	—Hades gave
14	—hell	—Hades

Chap.		Authorized Version.	Revised Version.
	14	—the second death.	—the second death, even the lake of fire.
	15	And whosoever	And if any
21	1	—there was no more sea.	—the sea is no more.
	2	—I John saw	—I saw
		—prepared	—made ready
	3	—heaven	—throne
		—his people,	—his peoples,
	4	And God shall wipe away all tears from their eyes; and there shall be no more death, neither sorrow nor crying, neither shall there be any more pain:	—and he shall wipe away every tear from their eyes; and death shall be no more; neither shall there be mourning, nor crying, nor pain, any more:
	5	—he said unto me, Write: for these words are true and faithful.	—he saith, Write: for these words are faithful and true.
	6	—It is done.	—They are come to pass.
	7	—all things;	—these things;
	8	—whoremongers,	—fornicators,
		—shall have their part	—their part shall be
	9	—the seven vials full of the seven last plagues, and talked with me,	—the seven bowls, who were laden with the seven last plagues; and he spake with me,
		—the Lamb's wife.	—the wife of the Lamb.
	10	—spirit	—Spirit
		—that great city, the Holy Jerusalem, descending	—the holy city Jerusalem, coming down

Chap.	Authorized Version.	Revised Version.
14	—in them the names	—on them twelve names
15	—he that talked with me had a golden reed to measure the city,	—he that spake with me had for a measure a golden reed to measure the city,
16	—the length is as large	—the length thereof is as great
18	—clear	—pure
19	—garnished	—adorned
20	—chrysoprasus;	—chrysoprase;
21	—every several gate	—each one of the several gates
22	—Lord God Almighty	—Lord God the Almighty,
	—of it.	—thereof.
23	—the Lamb is the light thereof.	—the lamp thereof is the Lamb.
24	—the nations of them which are saved shall walk in the light of it:	—the nations shall walk amidst the light thereof:
	—and honour	*omitted.*
25	—the gates of it shall not be shut at all by day:	—the gates thereof shall in no wise be shut by day
27	—that defileth, neither whatsoever worketh abomination, or maketh a lie: but they	—unclean, or he that maketh an abomination and a lie: but only they

22

1	—a pure river	—a river
	—clear	—bright
2	—on either side of the river,	—on this side of the river and on that
3	—no more curse:	—no curse any more:

Chap.	Authorized Version.	Revised Version.
3	—serve him:	—do him service;
5	—no night there; and they need no candle,	—night no more; and they need no light of lamp,
6	—of the holy prophets	—of the spirits of the prophets,
	—be done.	—come to pass.
7	—sayings (*Also in vv.* 9 *and* 10).	—words
8	—saw these things,	—am he that heard and saw these things.
11	He that is unjust, let him be unjust still: and he that is filthy, let him be filthy still: and he that is righteous, let him be righteous still: and he that is holy, let him be holy still.	He that is unrighteous, let him do unrighteousness still: and he that is filthy, let him be made filthy still: and he that is righteous, let him do righteousness still: and he that is holy, let him be made holy still.
12	—to give every man	—to render to each man
14	Blessed are they that do his commandments,	Blessed are they that wash their robes,
15	—whoremongers,	—fornicators,
16	—in the churches.	—for the churches.
17	—And whosoever will,	—he that will,
18	—add unto these things,	—add unto them,
19	—out of the book of life,	—from the tree of life,
	—and from the things which are written	—which are written
20	—Surely	—Yea:
	—Even so come,	—come,
21	The grace of our Lord Jesus Christ be with you all.	The grace of the Lord Jesus be with the saints.

www.ingramcontent.com/pod-product-compliance
Lightning Source LLC
Chambersburg PA
CBHW030324240426
43673CB00040B/1267